Student Teaching

Student Teaching

L. O. ANDREWS

Coordinator of Student Field Experience
College of Education
The Ohio State University

The Center for Applied Research in Education, Inc.
New York

Foreword

"While the Teaching Profession Slept," might well be the subtitle of this publication if its author were inclined more toward the melodramatic and less toward scholarship. In these pages L. O. Andrews presents an indictment, a warning, and a positive challenge to the profession of teaching. What he says is a frontal attack on complacency, slipshod scholarship, administrative expediency, and professional conservatism and provincialism. His prescription is the mobilization of talent, resources, knowledge, research, and practical skill to improve the preparation of teachers and thereby to raise the quality of American education.

The author offers the reader the rare gift of perspective. His years of experience as a college administrator of student-teaching programs and as a student of teacher education illumine his analysis of the problems and issues on student teaching, his discussion of the history and literature in the field, his projection of what lies ahead.

An exciting picture of what student teaching might and should be emerges from these pages. We see the imaginative use of new media to capture the behavior of teachers and learners in the classroom and to assist the prospective teacher in understanding and modifying his own behavior. We see a series of carefully planned, interrelated direct experiences as a part of a systematic five-year preservice program of teacher education and a true professional internship following this preservice program. We see schools, colleges, and state education agencies join forces to plan and conduct student teaching and internship programs in a spirit of genuine partnership. We see supervising teachers in the schools and college supervisors carefully selected, specifically prepared, and adequately compensated for their services. We see prospective teachers prepared to deal with change and equipped for a lifetime of professional development, and we see a teaching profession which has assumed increased responsibility for the quality of the preparation and practice of its members.

Along with the theoretical analysis, synthesis, and evaluation, the author includes much material that will be of immediate practical assistance to those currently responsible for student-teaching programs. For example, Chapter II includes a detailed summary of kinds of direct experiences and the purposes that each of these might be expected to serve in the collegiate program, and Chapter IV offers a thorough analysis of the roles of the supervising or cooperating teacher, the college supervisor and the school principal.

If this publication receives the thoughtful attention it deserves, by both public school and college personnel, it will produce constructive action by individuals and organizations and will take its place among the classic documents in the field of teacher education.

DON DAVIES
Executive Secretary

*National Commission on
    Teacher Education and
    Professional Standards*

Student Teaching

L. O. Andrews

Student teaching is a most important element in the preservice education of teachers. Universally, those who study the reactions of teachers to their preparation programs find that student teaching receives a lion's share of approval and approbation. Dr. James B. Conant in his recent book on *The Education of American Teachers* has singled out student teaching as the one aspect of teacher education where there is universal agreement.

This volume in the Library of Education will interest all those involved in the student-teaching process, including student teachers themselves, cooperating teachers in the schools, supervisors from the colleges and universities, and educational administrators. The book describes and evaluates student teaching today and suggests improvements needed to prepare for excellence in teaching. The book is based on L. O. Andrews' practical experience with student teaching programs and his keen insights as a leader in this important field.

WALTER A. ANDERSON
Content Editor

Contents

CHAPTER I

Student Teaching Today

In their educational programs many of the professions provide an opportunity for the neophyte to try his hand—to see how it feels to do the work of the professional practitioner. In the preparation of a teacher, student teaching has long been that initial experience; when the college student directs the learning of a group of pupils under the immediate observation of an experienced teacher. Success in student teaching is regularly accepted as evidence both of demonstrated performance and potential, and together with an adequate record in other requirements entitles the student to a recommendation for a teaching certificate.

Today, in most colleges, student teaching is not the only laboratory experience in teaching, but it remains the most frequently offered, usually the most extensive, and in the minds of students the most important. Over a century ago the founders of normal schools introduced student teaching (formerly and unfortunately often called practice teaching) as an integral part of the curriculum for the prospective elementary school teacher. During this century student teaching in secondary schools became a standard part of the professional curriculum in all types of colleges and universities. Special schools, known variously as model schools, practice schools, or laboratory schools, operated or controlled by the colleges, provided the setting for most student teaching up until 1900. Some colleges used college controlled schools for most of their student teaching until after World War II, while other colleges and universities not having campus schools had worked out arrangements with local public schools.

The shift to the use of public schools as laboratories for student teaching was progressing steadily when the many returning veterans of World War II swelled the ranks of student teachers so

1

rapidly that colleges had to seek the cooperation of many additional public schools immediately. Actually, neither college nor public school personnel ever had time to adapt their operations to this major shift before the exploding college enrollments of the late 1950's and early 1960's forced further rapid expansion of laboratory facilities, and college enrollments seem certain to double between 1960 and 1970. Barring some sharp changes in the economic, social, or international scene, or a decline in the proportion of college students entering teaching, the demand for student-teaching facilities should continue to rise sharply throughout the decade.

But alongside the problem of numbers and the shift to the use of public schools, student teaching itself has changed. Formerly the emphasis was on instruction alone; now students generally have contact with the many roles of the teacher. The time allocation has been increased both within the school day and in the number of weeks. Many students receive full-day assignments, a practice which is generally advocated because of the added realism, and because of the greater opportunity for professional development. Many colleges have adopted the full-time assignment primarily because they have to place their students in residential situations at considerable distances from the campus. Some colleges have been able to provide a series of laboratory experiences so that many of their students enter student teaching ready and anxious to take over major teaching responsibilities very quickly. Unfortunately, relatively few institutions have arranged significant post-student-teaching experiences. Despite the variety and extent of experiences introduced in various curricula, the beginning teacher still tends to find teaching even more strenuous than he expected and generally much more demanding than was true 20 or 40 years ago.

The literature dealing with student teaching and its many ramifications is expanding rapidly in quantity, if not always in quality. Even after a detailed analysis of this literature and the changes taking place in student teaching, three important questions would remain:

> 1. How effective are student teaching and other direct experiences in changing behavior and in getting students ready to serve as professional teachers?
> 2. How can schools and colleges combine forces to provide high

quality programs of student teaching and related experiences for
the expanding college enrollments?

3. What guides for the future development of these professional
experiences can be synthesized from historical trends, research findings and collective experience?

With the above questions as a guide, this monograph will review
the expanding field critically, develop several of the major issues,
and propose a rationale for improvement and further progress.

A Professional Paradox

Student teaching is the most universally approved education
course, both by educators and the general public—approved rather
generally even by the severest critics of professional teacher education. *Life Magazine* in an editorial criticizing teacher education
includes this evaluation: "Hardly anybody wants to do away with
'method' instruction altogether; on the contrary, practice-teaching
courses are extremely valuable."[1] Only very rarely does one find a
writer or professional committee recommending elimination of
student teaching or even a sharp reduction in either its extent or the
credit given for it. Usually students receive more credit for this
course than for any other in the professional sequence. Employ-
ing officials insist on having an evaluation of the student-teaching
experience in the placement office credentials of applicants. Where
letter grades are given, campus gossip often has it that an average
grade of "C" will positively kill one's chances for immediate employment as a teacher.

And yet storm warnings are going up. Very important people,
both within and without the profession, are viewing the persistent
problems of student teaching with deep concern and a few are
beginning seriously to question the effectiveness of much that is
called "student teaching." All this in spite of the fact that some
changes of a positive nature and some real progress are taking place.

No comprehensive national evaluation of student teaching and related experiences and their effectiveness has yet been made. Lack-
ing such studies, more informal and limited evidence must be
gathered to get a perspective for judgment. Throughout the later

---

[1] "Why Teachers Can't Teach," *Life Magazine* (March 22, 1963), p. 4.

chapters of this book various sources and types of evidence will be cited around three major concerns which seem fundamental to this paradox: failure to face fundamental issues, failure to solve persistent problems, and the inadequacy of research in this field.

Curiously enough it is easier to identify some of the causes for these failures and inadequacies than to determine the resulting effects of the limitations themselves. For example, persistent problems remain unsolved in the areas of operation and administration of programs in part because of the limited numbers of good public schools and well-qualified cooperating teachers available to many colleges, and in part because of the ridiculously limited budgets colleges are able to allocate to the entire student-teaching program. Public school teachers generally receive only a token payment for the added responsibility of directing the work of a student teacher —a task for which many have had no preparation and during which they often receive little assistance or direction from the college.

Everywhere the clamor is for higher quality teacher education, but the financial outlay for this purpose is disturbingly small. Thus, if the public really wants young professionals with demonstrated high competence, adequate financial support must be provided. An exact direct comparison between the cost of clinically-oriented medical education and present-day teacher education would be very difficult, but the often quoted figure that medical education is ten times as expensive is easily plausible. Numerous colleges do not compensate their cooperating teachers at all or give mere token payments, while many college supervisors are assigned two and three times the national standard of 20 student teachers as a full supervisory load.

The most comprehensive issue is how effective are student teaching and related experiences in meeting the objectives set up for them by college faculties. Early research, by means of correlating grades in student teaching with ratings of success in teaching, often produced very favorable results. But as the techniques of evaluation were refined the results proved to be disappointing. More recently the disturbing inadequacies of measures of teaching effectiveness have been carefully documented and widely publicized, although much more promising approaches are now being developed. Allen D. Patterson speaking at the 1939 meeting of the Supervisors of

Student Teaching (now the Association for Student Teaching) remarked, "It is almost trite to say that we cannot define the functions and values of student teaching until we agree upon what constitutes good teaching."[2] The dilemma remains just as real and almost as formidable today.

Some progress has been made in identifying objectives more sharply, refining the procedures for gathering and utilizing subjective judgments, and in research design. Research experts often state that newer techniques can be devised to get useful results without waiting for a simple definition of what constitutes good teaching. Admittedly the task is a difficult and complicated one, and progress seems certain to be painfully slow. But while waiting for research evidence and the development of new devices and procedures, the profession faces issues demanding immediate attention. Judgments must be made as to the worth of procedures now in use, the ways of attacking the many pressing problems, and the rationale to be followed in making both theoretical and practical decisions.

Diversity Unlimited

Uniformity and standardization of pattern and program definitely are not characteristics of student teaching in America today. Until the 1930's students normally were assigned for one hour a day in the elementary schools or one period a day in high schools for all or most of a semester, and usually in campus laboratory schools or local public schools where the emphasis was primarily on instruction of pupils. But during the 1930's a considerable number of college faculties concerned themselves with improving the quality of teacher education and they pioneered a variety of innovations in student teaching and related experiences, including several types of post-degree, post-certification internships. After World War II changes did occur, but many were dictated of necessity because of the greater numbers of potential teachers, the lack of local laboratory facilities, a desire for greater realism in experiences, and

---

[2] Supervisors of Student Teaching, *Report of Nineteenth Annual Session. Cleveland, February 27 and 28, 1939*, p. 37. This report is considered The Eighteenth Yearbook of the Supervisors of Student Teaching, now the AST.

changes in the teacher-education curricula in the post-Sputnik era.

Some trends and general developments are clearly evident or can be charted with some confidence, but the striking fact is the great variety and wide range that exists in the qualitative and quantitative aspects of these professional experiences.

Most surveys show that nearly 1200 colleges offer teacher-education curricula and almost all offer credit courses in student teaching. These institutions include the widest variety of types: publicly supported teachers colleges (formerly called normal schools and now rapidly changing to state colleges or universities), state colleges, universities, and municipal colleges; liberal arts colleges, the private universities, and a few privately supported teachers colleges, and some junior colleges and university branches which offer a few professional courses. Students earn from two to twenty or more semester hours of credit in student teaching and are assigned in a school from one period (or hour) a day for part of a term to full days for more than a semester. Very few colleges still use campus schools exclusively as laboratories for student teaching, but many colleges use a combination of on- and off-campus laboratory schools, nearby public schools, and even some schools or centers at great distances from the campus.

In some colleges student teaching is the most responsible experience of a carefully designed series of professional experiences, while at other colleges it may be the only such experience provided. Two states (Oregon and Connecticut) have defined the legal status of a student teacher by law, while another state (California) authorizes the county superintendent to issue student-teaching certificates. Most colleges assign a college staff member to supervise a given group of student teachers, while a few institutions apparently turn over the complete responsibility for supervision to the public school authorities. Some school systems sharply limit the amount of full-responsibility teaching which a student teacher is permitted to do, while other districts require that the classroom teacher remain in the room at all times while the student teacher is teaching. At the other extreme, there are some campus schools where student teachers do virtually all of the teaching.

At least eight states have formal certification standards for supervising teachers, while others have no criteria at all for teachers who will direct the work of student teachers. Several states have developed a very comprehensive approach to student teaching by providing leadership for the cooperative efforts of the state department of education, the colleges, the public schools, and the state education associations. Efforts of this type have been in progress for many years in California and Kentucky, for example, while special cooperative study programs are now in progress in West Virginia and North Carolina. Georgia has the most comprehensive state program for certifying supervising teachers. It also provides in-service training for this special function at three levels, and compensates the approved teachers, on a graduated basis, from state funds. Most colleges have tried, within the limit of their resources, to recognize and compensate the teachers and administrators who work with prospective teachers. As a result payment to teachers or directly to the district varies from no payment to $300 and more per student teacher, and the variety of "fringe" benefits is also quite varied. These include recognition in the college catalog, and privileges such as free tuition, use of the library, athletic tickets, use of clinics for special pupils, special funds for extra teaching material, and honoraria and expenses to attend special campus meetings and conferences.

Nowhere are the vast extremes between excellence and inadequacy in student teaching more striking and more shocking than in the dimension of quality. Some student teachers have a skillfully guided growth experience which leads them to an artistic and professionally effective performance in directing learning, while others have a continuously frustrating, emotionally disturbing experience during which they receive little positive direction or assistance, and may in fact learn unwise and professionally unsound procedures. Annually thousands of student teachers find themselves assigned under teachers who hold ideas quite at variance with those taught in their college courses, and sometimes these teachers are guilty of serious breaches of professional ethics.

Two or three decades ago, most of the teachers in both on- and off-campus laboratory schools were carefully selected, outstanding teachers who were extremely skillful in directing the work of student teachers. Today numerous public school teachers have also become skilled in working with student teachers, but over 200,000 such teachers are needed every year to work with college students. Most of these teachers have a student teacher only once a year, and probably a majority have never had any course or planned in-service instruction in the supervision of a student teacher—a task which combines the roles of a personnel director and a guidance counselor with that of a superior classroom teacher. Some colleges have an adequate number of able supervising teachers readily available, but too many others are like a certain state college which annually places 600 student teachers in a territory of about 120 miles in diameter. There the director of student teaching is forced to use every certificated teacher who can possibly be persuaded to accept a student teacher, regardless of teaching ability.

Few educators in any segment of the profession object to freedom for institutions to experiment, to explore new patterns, to modify programs, and to adapt their procedures to conditions as they find them. Unlimited diversity in this or other areas of teacher education, however, can scarcely be considered a strength of American teacher education. Programs judged to be excellent do exist and the record of graduates from them often seems to bear out their claim of quality, but the great diversity still remains. If college enrollments were stationary or declining, some encouragement could be taken in the hope that with modest continuing progress substantial gains would occur over a period of time.

Unless all signs fail, the fears of many directors and coordinators seem well founded—that the quality of student teaching will not improve generally, actually will decline in various places, unless and until the profession as a whole recognizes the dimensions of the problem and takes effective action. Many of the long-time observers and leaders in this field are convinced that few colleges and individual public school systems can really solve their problems alone and unaided. National recognition and study are definitely needed, but action probably will have to come on a state-by-state basis through the cooperative effort of many professional and official agencies.

Definition of Terms

Not so disturbing, perhaps, but just as striking is the diversity in terminology used in this area of direct experiences for prospective teachers. Practices differ sharply in certain states and often among different institutions within the same state. The Association for Student Teaching, through its Committee on Terminology, prepared and distributed a small bulletin in the late 1950's on *Selected Terminology* as defined and recommended for use by the committee. Perhaps the most significant impact on terminology was made by the 1948 publication of *School and Community Laboratory Experiences in Teacher Education*.[3] The definitions which follow are adapted from those found in these two publications and will form the basis for usage in this book:

Professional laboratory experiences. All those contacts with children, youth, and adults in school and community, including observation, participation, teaching, and other leadership activities which make a direct contribution to an understanding of basic concepts and principles as well as of individuals and their guidance in the teaching-learning process.

Student teaching. A period of guided teaching when a college student assumes increasing responsibility for directing the learning of a group or groups of learners over a period of consecutive weeks.

Directed observation. Those opportunities provided for students to see teaching, learning, and all manner of community activities without necessarily becoming involved in the on-going activity itself.

Participation. Those experiences of the college student in which he takes an active part, under direction, in an on-going teaching, learning, or other community activity. Also defined as all those activities along a continuum between observation and full responsibility for teaching or directing the activities of a group in a school or other community agency.

Student teacher. A college student who is engaged in an assigned student-teaching experience, but the term is often used to refer to any college student preparing to teach. Recently the term *associate teacher* is being suggested as a more useful designation for a student who takes over the full responsibility for directing the learning of groups of pupils.

---

[3] Sub-Committee of the Standards and Surveys Committee, *School and Community Laboratory Experiences in Teacher Education* (Oneonta, N.Y.: American Association of Teachers Colleges, 1948), pp. 7 and 197 particularly.

Supervising teacher or cooperating teacher.   A teacher of school pupils who also directs the work of a student teacher with these same pupils.

The Association for Student Teaching accepts only the term *supervising teacher,* since the Association prefers an umbrella term covering both the laboratory school teacher and the public school teacher working with student teachers. In practice many colleges and school systems find this term confusing when used along with *college supervisor* and thus prefer to use the differentiating term of *cooperating teacher* for a teacher in a cooperating public school. Only rarely is the term *sponsor teacher* used, even though many consider it to have the most positive and the least negative connotations. The designation, *teacher education associate,* has been proposed as a term to be used in recognizing the demonstrably competent *sponsor teacher.* Historically this teacher-function of directing a student teacher has been designated by a great number of terms, many of which were most unfortunate, such as, model teacher, master teacher, directing teacher, and probably worst of all, critic teacher, which became an official rank title in many colleges and a part of state certification terminology.

College supervisor.   A regular college staff member who has as a part or all of his assigned work load the supervision of the activities of student teachers and the relationships and conditions under which these students carry on their work. Because of the variety of off-campus student-teaching situations, several other terms have come into common use, such as, *off-campus supervisor, resident supervisor, resident coordinator,* or *area supervisor,* and these sometimes refer to local school personnel or others employed by the college either part-time or full-time for this specific function only.

Other members of the student teaching team.   Increasing attention is being given to defining the role of other professional personnel involved in providing high quality professional laboratory experiences and student teaching. In the public schools those most directly involved are *principals, supervisors,* and *superintendents,* especially at the policy-making level, various special service personnel, and in larger systems some designated person who serves as a *coordinator of teacher-education services,* regardless of the actual title carried. Most colleges designate a *director* or *coordinator of student teaching,* and occasionally a *coordinator of professional laboratory* or *field experiences* who is responsible for more than student teaching, per se. Even apart from the central administration of the institution, the depth of understanding and the decisions made by the responsible department chairman and the appropriate academic dean are very important to the whole program of professional laboratory experiences.

Laboratory school. A school, either on or off campus, in which the operation, curriculum, functions or selection of staff, or any combination of these, are controlled wholly or in part by the college. Originally most laboratory schools were private, nonpublic schools, but a considerable number, especially some of the larger ones, are operated jointly by the college and a local school system. Formerly the function of one of these schools was to serve primarily as a laboratory for student teaching, or for observation, participation, and student teaching. Some schools are used as centers for experimentation, program development and research, or for some combination of these and related teacher-education functions.

Cooperating school and cooperating school district. A school or school system which provides facilities for professional laboratory experiences for college students, but which is neither controlled nor supported by the college. Ideally the school district has a written working agreement with the college, setting forth the conditions under which these activities are to be conducted together with the benefits and privileges extended in both directions.

Internship. The definition of *internship* and of *intern* are among the most controversial of all of the terms. This writer prefers to accept the concept developed by research late in the 1930's when many city and college programs were designed and put into operation. Thus, *internship* is that period in the total program of teacher education when a college graduate, having completed formal teacher education and holding an initial certificate, is employed part-time up to one year, receives a salary proportionate to his service, is supervised primarily by the school system but with a continuing relationship with college personnel, and follows a planned study program designed to produce a demonstrably competent, professional teacher. Unfortunately the term *internship* is also used in various parts of the country to refer to full-time, off-campus student teaching, as well as to a period of initial professional experience as a part of a fifth-year program leading to initial certification.

Apprenticeship or apprentice teaching. These terms are also used with a variety of meanings. The dictionary definition and common usage outside of the teaching profession give a basis for the following definition: *Apprenticeship* is that period of employed service when a student combines his initial professional study with teaching experience as a means of qualifying for initial certification under a combined earn and learn plan. At present most *apprentice teaching* plans enroll college graduates who have had only a very brief period of professional study, such as a summer school program, prior to entering full-time teaching service.

Clinical experience.   For its use in this book, *clinical experience* is defined somewhat as in medicine—carefully planned student contact with individuals and very small groups of learners under the direct supervision of skilled practitioners with the student making diagnoses, prognoses, and projecting treatment plans for individuals with learning problems. At first the instruction (treatment) would be given by the expert teachers and later by the students under supervision. The term *clinical* is sometimes used to refer to all the direct experiences with children, youth, and adults interchangeably with the term, *professional laboratory experiences.* The other form, *clinics,* has been used to refer to conferences held by the Association for Student Teaching (as well as by other organizations and agencies) during which the attendants critically examine in whole or in part the teacher-education curriculum of the host college.

Summary

Today student teaching and professional laboratory experiences comprise a very complex group of activities supported by a large and growing group of professionals who perform a wide variety of roles and functions. The terminology and diversity are confusing and disturbing. Historically a great deal of thought, study, research, and dedicated effort has brought the field to its present level of development; and the increased interest in further study, research, and improvement is definitely very encouraging. Much more intensive effort must be put forth if the full potential of direct experiences in teacher education is to be realized.

CHAPTER II

Direct Experience in Teacher Education

Oversimplification of a concept may prove helpful at times, but it may also lull the user into a quick acceptance of an inadequate point of view. The colloquial version of one of Dewey's philosophical positions—we learn by doing—may very well have been accepted by many as adequate proof of the value of student teaching. If this were not the case, perhaps the literature would contain more careful analyses of the value of student teaching and other experiences. Informal lists of purposes do appear frequently in publications such as handbooks for student teachers, college catalogs, and bulletins for students, but penetrating analyses of objectives are rare. By contrast, an extensive literature considers the proper organization of student teaching, how it should be conducted, the activities that should be included, and the role of the cooperating teacher. Indeed, this whole area has evolved largely under the impact of pragmatic pressures, rather than from any generally accepted theoretical base.

Evolving Practices and Concepts

Historically, student teaching appears to have consisted of imitation and repeated practice of a particular method taught by the normal school professor and demonstrated in the classroom by the "model" teacher. At the secondary level the earliest student teaching may have been even more subject centered than today, since some early records show that the cooperative arrangements were made with teachers of specific subjects, such as botany, Latin, mathematics, and the like, rather than with high schools or school systems. Courses in student teaching antedate the development of

14

educational psychology, the whole testing movement, and research in child development; and thus, the early patterns seem narrow both in conception and practice.

Until 1920 student teaching was a practical, vocationally-oriented course regularly required in the elementary curriculum of normal schools; but student teaching at the high school level was offered and accepted for credit in relatively few universities, in fewer liberal arts colleges, but routinely in those normal schools which had introduced secondary education curricula. Since colonial times a substantial proportion of the graduates of liberal arts colleges had become teachers in academies and high schools without benefit of professional courses. Such college faculties had a strong aversion to offering student teaching at all and were especially opposed to giving credit for it toward a degree.

But in the years from 1920–40 student teaching was almost literally legislated into the curriculum of most four-year colleges and universities, because many states adopted laws or regulations requiring professional courses, student teaching, and a degree for certification to teach in high schools. Faced with the possible loss of students to the developing teachers colleges, the faculties of many liberal arts colleges and universities promptly introduced professional courses, including student teaching, and accepted the credit toward degree requirements.

During this same period professional organizations began to exert considerable influence on student teaching. Before 1900 only groups of normal school personnel seem to have taken much interest and done much writing in this field. The National Society of College Teachers of Education was organized in 1902, but its concern in this specific area declined so much that a small group broke away in 1920 and formed the Supervisors of Student Teaching, which later became the Association for Student Teaching. For more than two decades this association published the proceedings of their annual meetings and now, for a similar period, their yearbooks have been written by committees, generally on a theme or single topic. These yearbooks together with the Association's minor publications form a major source of information in this field.

In 1917 an organization of institutions, the American Association of Teachers Colleges, was formed, and its 1926 yearbook carries the text of its first standards for member institutions. They were quantitative in nature, as were most standards at that time, but they did set a minimum of 90 clock hours of student teaching for graduates of teachers colleges. Later the 90 hours of direct experiences were equated with five semester hours of credit.

The decade of the "Great Depression," the 1930's, provided the social and educational climate for the development of many new concepts and practices in teacher education. College enrollments rose as many unemployed but able young people managed to find ways to stay in school, and for the first time the country had an oversupply of degree-holding, certificated teachers, although only at the high school level. College faculties, in an effort to improve the competence of their graduates, devised a wide variety of new experiences in schools, in community agencies and organizations, and in various kinds of community study. Research on child growth and development flourished, and the growing momentum of this movement may very well have influenced faculty ideas about teaching experiences. Elaborate programs of pre-student teaching activities and some post-student teaching experiences, including a great variety of different activities, were conceived and explored. Some representative samples of the more important types will be noted here.

Separate courses in observation had been common in normal schools, but faculties became disenchanted with the apparent poor results. Education professors joined campus school teachers in developing various patterns of assigned observation-participation experiences as an integral part of regular professional courses, which ranged from initial courses to more advanced methods classes. Ideally the students were to undertake more involved and responsible activities as their knowledge increased, and the classroom was expected to serve as the laboratory to illuminate the theory of the college course. Some colleges were able to make satisfactory arrangements for similar activities in public schools despite the many difficulties involved.

The faculty at The Ohio State University took advantage of the late opening of campus classes to design the "September Field Experience Program" which permits students to have a two or three week full-time, general school exploratory experience in a public school. The students serve as volunteer assistants at a busy time of year, see the school open, and observe the over-all operation of a school while usually getting deeply involved in the classroom instruction of one or two teachers.

The search for laboratory experiences to supplement textbooks and class learning about child growth and development, and community life and problems prompted the design and exploration of a great variety of nonschool experiences. A course given at the University of Wisconsin, "The Child: His Nature and Needs," had an accompanying leadership experience in many different community agencies, such as settlement houses, YMCAs, scout troops, day nurseries, and Sunday schools. Wayne State University developed its 200 hour program of leadership experiences in nonschool agencies as a part of the requirements for admission to upperclass professional study. Students in a course at the former Albany State Teachers College in New York would spend a few days as a class, studying a community intensively under the immediate direction of the professor.

The most striking development of this period was the emergence of internship programs in some 40 cities, some of which were designed and operated jointly by school systems and teacher-preparation institutions. The oversupply of certificated teachers plus the emphasis on quality and innovation produced a favorable climate for the sudden emergence of this new internship experience. At the same time the large number of degree-holding persons seeking initial certification prompted institutions such as the University of Michigan and the Bank Street College of Education in New York City to design short, concentrated professional programs, sometimes including a "block type," short full-time student teaching arrangement.

Following World War II the teacher shortage continued, especially at the elementary school level where it was accentuated by the increase in enrollments due to the rapid rise in the birth rate. Under pressures from many quarters, colleges devised a wide variety of emergency programs. Of these the best publicized were those in which holders of liberal arts degrees were able to fulfill the requirements for certification and at some colleges obtain an M.A.T. (Master of Arts in Teaching) degree at the same time. As a part of these plans several types of experiences were devised, including special student teaching in summer schools both before or after teaching experience, full-time apprenticeship teaching, and various modifications of full-time student teaching during a year of intensive professional study. Included in some programs, especially some of the M.A.T. plans, were extensive experiences as a member of a group engaged in team teaching.

Most observers would agree that the most significant publication in this field was *School and Community Laboratory Experiences in Teacher Education*[1] issued in 1948 by the American Association of Teachers Colleges. (It is often referred to as the Flowers Report, named for the chairman of the Sub-Committee, John G. Flowers.) Combining as it did principles, issues, extensive reports of practice and suggested standards, it also projected an image of what a good program ought to include. Its impact on thought and discussion has been considerable, but the effect on practice appears to have been less marked, probably because of the practical problems involved in realizing these objectives and because of later developments, such as the recent pressure to reduce professional courses.

Some have suggested that colleges tried to follow the report too literally as if it were a blue print. In the opinion of others, the recommended standards set a goal which was beyond the combined resources of many colleges and their local school and community facilities. The distinctive contribution of the report is that it surveyed the varied developments of the 1930's, organized them into trends and patterns, and dramatized the potentialities of professional laboratory experiences.

The continuing shift to the use of off-campus public schools for student teaching is now so complete that most new teachers have had at least some of their experiences, and many have had all, in public schools, and have experienced many of the complex roles of a public school teacher. Unfortunately, the shift brought losses too. Most cooperating teachers work with just one student teacher at a time eliminating the valuable learning which occurred when

---

[1] Sub-Committee of the Standards and Surveys Committee, *School and Community Laboratory Experiences in Teacher Education* (Oneonta, N.Y.: American Association of Teachers Colleges, 1948).

two or more students worked together. Even with the most effective selection procedures it is virtually impossible to find enough public school teachers who are as skillful in working with student teachers as the typical experienced laboratory school teacher.

Some observers assumed that by the middle 1960's virtually all student teaching would be on a full-day basis, but the post-Sputnik period brought a heated re-examination of teacher education. Pressures quickly built up to increase the amount of general education and the required work in the teaching subject areas. Since the total credit requirements for the four-year degree are relatively fixed, reductions were made in the electives and in the professional courses, thus often reducing or effectively preventing any expansion in student teaching.

The professional standards movement spearheaded by the National Commission on Teacher Education and Professional Standards (TEPS) had campaigned vigorously to get the bachelor's degree recognized as the basic minimum for all certification and thereby eliminate the subdegree programs for elementary school teachers. Thus, it was natural that these several influences would stimulate discussion of the desirability of requiring five years of college for initial certification. Three states have instituted this plan and several institutions have pilot programs covering five years which contain a two-year general education foundation plus a three-year professional plan, sometimes referred to as the MA–3 plan—three years from sophomore standing to a master's degree. These plans are in addition to the common fifth-year certification program for degree holders.

Thus student teaching and other direct experiences in teacher education have evolved to the mid-1960's. The problems resulting from the expanding enrollments, the desirability of requiring five years for initial certification, the need for internships, plus the constant struggle to develop and maintain high quality experiences are some of the chief concerns of those who are responsible for student teaching and related experiences.

The Contributions of
Professional Laboratory Experiences

Neither formal research nor theoretical statements give much assistance in identifying the effects of the use of direct experiences as an integral part of the teacher-education curriculum. Many informal studies reveal the values which student teachers report they gained through these experiences, and students have generally rated student teaching very high in comparison with other courses. Supervisors of long experience become keen observers of student behavior and development even though their judgments are subjective. Such evidence as this ought to be carefully refined into precise hypotheses, which then could be tested through research. The findings from such research would certainly serve as more useful guides to designers of teacher-education curricula than anything now available for that purpose.

The informal statements from manuals, handbooks, syllabi, and similar minor publications are usually couched in the form of objectives for courses such as student teaching. Many of these purposes of student teaching can, perhaps, be synthesized into three types of goals, which would also include those generally accepted by students:

1. To provide for a concentrated period of growth in professional and personal attributes, understandings, and skills of the teacher.
2. To assist a student to discover if teaching is what he really wants to do, and actually can do.
3. To permit a student to demonstrate that his ability and potential warrant recommendation for a teaching certificate.

Most student teachers seek answers to those all important questions, "Can I teach?" and "Will I like teaching?" Thus, the second objective of self-realization is basic even though some students with the richest backgrounds of varied experience may feel they have affirmative answers. Probably all persons involved in teacher education accept the third objective, the evaluative aspect of student teaching, but the issue is whether this is to be the dominant objective. There is a school of thought which takes the position that students should learn how to teach in their professional courses and demonstrate the adequacy of their learning in student teaching.

This position is not now commonly held in America but it is still the basis for the practice in other countries where students must demonstrate their competence in teaching certain lessons to unfamiliar classes before a jury of evaluators.

Both the literature and the practice of the present day indicate that the first purpose is fundamental—education for the broad general objective of professional growth. Several of the historical shifts in emphasis tend to support this view: the extension of time to allow for greater maturation, contact with more of the roles of the teacher, more concern for professional and personal development, and greater emphasis on self-evaluation.

The most widely recognized set of principles are the nine given in the first chapter of the Flowers Report. Only the first of these is devoted entirely to the contribution of direct experiences, and is stated thus:

> Principle I. The particular contribution of professional laboratory experiences (including student teaching) to the education of teachers is three-fold: (1) an opportunity to implement theory— both to study the pragmatic value of the theory and to check with the student his understanding of the theory in application; (2) a field of activity which, through raising questions and problems, helps the student to see his needs for further study; and (3) an opportunity to study with the student his ability to function effectively when guiding actual teaching-learning situations.[2]

By contrast the other eight principles are not affirmations of this type but rather projections of the way the Sub-Committee thought professional laboratory experiences *should* be conducted. Presumably these statements represent a synthesis of the best practices discovered in the survey and the convictions of the Committee members themselves. All of the principles were generally well accepted by the large panel of consultants which reviewed the Committee's first draft of the report.

Two of the other nine principles include reference to specific objectives and thus implied contributions of professional laboratory experiences. Principle III urges extensive guided contact with learners and concludes, "to contribute to functional understanding of human growth and development."[3] Similarly, Principle IV directs

2 *Ibid.,* p. 16.
3 *Ibid.,* p. 23.

that experiences should be designed "to afford opportunity for responsible participation in all of the important phases of the teacher's activities, both in and out of school."[4] The text following these principles does suggest some reasons for such recommendations, but the principles themselves only imply the contribution of such broad experiences.

The literature of philosophy of education and related areas includes analyses of the function and meaning of direct and indirect or vicarious experiences in teacher education, but seldom do writings on teacher education and student teaching, per se, deal critically and in depth with this problem. One of the exceptions is a section of a chapter by Stratemeyer in *Teacher Education for a Free People*.[5] Even there, however, the contributions of direct experience are developed in relation to teacher education in general rather than to student teaching and laboratory experiences. Her analysis of the two types of experiences concludes with this significant summarization:

> For verbal pursuits to have action concepts there must be concrete imagery which is exact and accurate. This suggests that when the student has not had previous direct contact with the situations and concepts under consideration or with similar or related events, direct experience should be provided if at all possible. When there has been pertinent previous direct experience, vivid and accurate imagery can be a part of vicarious experience.[6]

The absence of more comprehensive analyses of the contribution of direct experience poses a very real dilemma for the designer of professional courses for prospective teachers. Surely all these varied experiences, which have now been conceived and explored, do not and will not each make the same contribution to the development of a competent professional. The rapid shift of the locale of the professional laboratory to the public school and community forces a redesign of those experiences which had been so often provided in more restricted laboratory schools and immediate college neighborhoods. The literature on curriculum construc-

[4] *Ibid.*, p. 26.
[5] Florence B. Stratemeyer, "Issues and Problems in Teacher Education," in *Teacher Education for a Free People,* Donald P. Cottrell, ed. (Oneonta, N.Y.: American Association of Colleges for Teacher Education, 1956), pp. 62–73.
[6] *Ibid.*, p. 69.

tion for the public school suggests that the initial stage is to list the desired outcomes of any proposed curriculum. But often the education professor seems prone to request a certain kind and amount of experience as a part of a given course, rather than to identify any carefully developed set of desired outcomes or needs of his students.

Until a more comprehensive theoretical base is available, the practical alternative is to develop a set of hypothetical objectives and possible contributions of all types of direct experiences in professional teacher education. Limited experience with such a list suggests that it is possible to design specific experiences which stand up well upon informal evaluation by students and staff. The most surprising outcome is that some carefully designed experiences are very effective even though ridiculously short, as compared with the constant pressure over the last three decades to provide more numerous and more extensive experiences. The list which follows represents an informal composite of the accumulated subjective judgment of many faculty members, who have designed experiences for their students, given them extensive trial, and evaluated the results through their own and their students' eyes. Assuredly these hoped for outcomes should be subjected to rigorous research, but they are presented here as a useful practical tool for course design.

Many direct experiences currently included in teacher-education curricula are thought to contribute to the education of a teacher in one or more of the following ways:

1. Providing a basis for a *personal decision* to become or not to become a teacher.
2. Developing *readiness* for professional courses, professional experiences, professional growth, and for full-responsibility teaching.
3. Developing mature *professional purposes* and *attitudes*.
4. Strengthening understanding by exposure to *reality* which adds *feeling* and other *sensory impressions* to verbalized knowledge.
5. Providing an opportunity to *acquire, use,* and *test information*.
6. Developing professional *understanding* of *concepts* and *theories* from professional and related disciplines.
7. Developing *skill* in the use of *professional techniques*.
8. Developing *insight* and *judgment* in applying professional knowledge.

9. Providing a basis for evaluating *professional, social,* and *personal* growth.
10. Providing a feeling of significant personal worth—the satisfaction that comes from *giving useful professional service.*

At the conclusion of the next section these objectives are presented in chart form with an indication of the types of experiences which should contribute to each outcome.

Types of Experiences

Direct experiences currently in use in teacher education are grouped here under five main headings to facilitate the classification of the great number of different kinds. Two of the five types are further broken down into two subtypes each. The whole scheme was developed to assist in the design of curricula and experiences in teacher education. The following listing includes some of the characteristics and potential uses of each type.

Observation. The value of an observation depends, of course, upon what is seen, but also, to a very great extent, upon the previous experience of the viewer and his sophistication and ability to perceive the less obvious. Carefully directed observations for which the viewer has been well prepared usually prove more profitable to students than those which are random and undirected. Long continued observations of teaching-learning situations, without more active involvement, become very boring to students and the law of diminishing returns radically reduces the learning therefrom.

Observation—direct. First-hand observations in schools and communities add the touch of reality to textbook and other verbalized knowledge. But shortly after the first few contacts have been completed the instructor is faced with increasing problems in directing the observations profitably. This is especially true since it is so seldom that a whole class can see exactly the same thing as a prelude to class discussion and analysis. There is always the very real question of whether or not observers will actually see what they came to observe and whether or not the lesson will be worth observing.

Observation—reproductions via the new media. Many different approaches have been used in an effort to arrange for entire classes to see a single teaching situation, such as constructing large laboratory school classrooms, observation booths, and one way screens or glass. With the electronic age new media make possible the transmission of a reproduction of a classroom episode to almost any size of college class. But even closed circuit television does not change the transitory character of a teacher-directed lesson, for it is a "now you see it, now it's gone, never to be recreated again" type of phenomenon.

Capturing a live class on film is a costly process, and has seldom proved very successful by either educational or technical standards. Recording classroom activity on video tape (teletape) costs must less than three camera photography, and with three remote controlled television cameras and proper monitoring the resulting teletape can be of both high technical and professional quality. It is now possible to transfer this teletape recording to 16 millimeter sound film (an advanced type of kinescope), preserving much of the high quality and providing greater permanence and more flexibility. The industry predicts that the same process will soon be possible with the much more economical eight millimeter sound film when it has been made compatible for use with both closed and open circuit television.

Therefore, it is now technically possible for institutions to build a large library of faithful reproductions of all types and levels of classroom episodes, good and bad. These can be used on television circuits or shown on a screen with a projector for all types and levels of pre-service and in-service teacher education. A library of carefully selected, classified, cataloged, and annotated reproductions of teaching-learning will provide teacher educators with a new resource of almost unlimited potential. Several institutions are exploring these processes, and with some leadership in coordinating their efforts this idea can become a reality in a few years.

Participation. Not uncommonly, prospective teachers urge their professors to give them something practical, something they can use. And then many will resist vigorously having a new experience in which they may find themselves challenged—even frightened a bit—because they have never done these things before and do not feel equipped to meet the situation. Upon concluding participation experiences students generally are most enthusiastic, even some of the previously reluctant ones now say emphatically that every student should be required to have the experience. Professors find their classes enriched by the questions and problems brought back by the students, and, when carefully designed, these experiences seem to add much to the students' growth in understanding.

Participation in schools. When assigned for observation and participation in a classroom, students appreciate the opportunity to be active and to have even a small part in the teaching. Relatively young teachers are often most effective in directing the activities of participants because they seem intuitively to appreciate the real needs of such students. The potential activities are many but from the beginning should be well selected from four different types: observing, carrying out noninstructional routines, assisting the teacher both in and out of class with the ongoing instructional activity, and carrying out small, unitary, and exploratory teaching activities sometimes referred to as "bit" teaching.

These are not "flunky" activities to exploit the student as cheap labor, but rather real teaching responsibilities necessitating neither transitions nor formal lesson plans. Though brief, the impact upon the student and upon his readiness and understanding in his campus courses may be very high. The level of responsibility in participation activities can be adjusted readily to the demonstrated competence of the individual and to courses varying from introductory to the most advanced.

Participation in the community. Experiences observing and participating in the community are even more diverse and less well defined than those in schools. The two most persistent elements are contacts with different communities, socioeconomic levels and cultures, and leadership experiences with children and youth, especially in recreational, social, welfare, and camp settings. Those who have directed students in such leadership roles tend to believe that this type of activity has more potential to change young people, their behavior, attitudes, and purposes than any other type which has thus far been developed. The essential element seems to be to place a student in a new social group long enough for him to identify himself with the new group, accept their purposes as his purposes, their needs as his responsibility, and get satisfaction from feeling that his efforts make a difference in their lives.

Unfortunately, only a relatively small per cent of colleges preparing teachers provide rich community experiences, including, also, those that build an understanding of the roles of other agencies and disciplines; and in many programs there is little if any supervision by college personnel and no accompanying seminar. Even very intense and stimulating experiences may provide little real professional growth and understanding unless they are accompanied by some type of group session providing some intellectualization of the experience and its implications.

Student teaching. A temporary delegation of most of the roles of the teacher to a college student is the central element in student teaching and it remains the heart of most programs of direct experience. While the nature of the assignment would usually remain the same, still different patterns of experiences might suggest drastic changes in the functions of student teaching itself. If, by chance, the emerging pattern should become that of providing not just student teaching *or* internship, but student teaching *plus* internship, then student teaching could become preparatory, and not the terminal experience, thus producing readiness for rigorous professional courses and the later internship. This is the view of student teaching which is analyzed in the table at the end of this section, and is actually the primary function of the modified, summer student teaching placed just before full-time apprenticeship in some fifth-year programs.

Clinical experiences. Proposed here as an addition to this list of types of direct experience in teacher education, clinical experiences—defined as in medical school curricula—have scarcely ever been clearly designed, much less explored in depth. Extensive case studies of individual pupils once were commonly assigned in student teaching, but now such activity is used more functionally to undergird remedial work. Child study clinics, and even some treatment clinics, operate on many campuses and in many school systems with teacher-education students often serving primarily as observers and assistants, and only very occasionally becoming more deeply involved. But few current clinical situations, except those in institutions for disturbed or delinquent children, could provide the quality of experiences sought under the definition given in the previous chapter.

If, when a student had completed brief introductory courses and a readiness type of student teaching, he would take senior and graduate level courses in methods, the educational foundations, and the related disciplines, then the clinical experiences could serve as the laboratory activities for these courses. The clinic should permit him to study individuals and small groups of pupils with real learning problems. He should make detailed diagnoses, prognoses, and propose treatment which would usually be given by the teacher in charge, but the student might be allowed to have a part in the treatment phase of the teaching later. In addition, the student would observe and confer with the practitioners in the related disciplines and be invited to all "staffing" sessions when his pupil subjects were being studied cooperatively by psychiatrists, psychologists, social case workers, teachers, and others.

The rationale behind this proposal involves a recognition of the impossibility of raising beginning teachers to the level of real scholarship in the related disciplines and also in the professional subject areas themselves. But advanced students having clinical experiences concurrently should find their rate of learning and level of understanding sharply increased in their theoretical courses.

The evidence strongly suggests that students who have had extensive work with individual learners prior to student teaching, or teachers who have studied children under the direction of capable child psychologists, are usually very sensitive to individual needs when teaching full classes. Teachers of the educationally disadvantaged and of the many types of children in special classes should find clinical experiences a valuable contribution to their preparation, because, although they cannot provide the specialized service of the other disciplines themselves, they must understand their possible contribution. Exploration of the possibility of using clinical experiences in the preparation of regular teachers should also be undertaken, and this total area promises to be a fertile field for research.

Internship. Sharply differentiated from apprenticeship as an introductory experience for initial certification, internship would be the culminating experience of a carefully structured sequence. The emphasis would be on consolidating one's skill as a teacher and on developing higher levels of professional understanding, insight, and judgment. Hopefully, upon the completion of such an experience, most students would have demonstrated a substantial level of professional competence and readiness to begin giving professional service and to embark upon a long-time program of professional growth.

SOME POSSIBLE OBJECTIVES TO BE REALIZED FROM
DIFFERENT EXPERIENCES IN PROFESSIONAL TEACHER EDUCATION

	Observation— Direct	Observation— Reproductions via new media	Participation— School	Participation— Community	Student Teaching	Clinical	Internship
1. Decision on Teaching Career	I	S	P	P	S		I
2. Readiness	I	S	P	P	P	I	I
3. Purposes and Attitudes	I	S	S	P	S	P	S
4. Reality and Feeling	P	S	S	S	S	P	I
5. Acquisition and Test of Information		P	P	S	P	S	S
6. Understanding of Theories and Concepts	S	P	S	S	S	P	S
7. Professional Skill		I	S	I	S	I	P
8. Insight and Judgment			I	I	S	S	P
9. Professional and Personal Growth			S	S	P	S	P
10. Feeling of Personal Worth			I	P	I	I	I

Code: P—primary objective,   S—secondary objective,   I—incidental learning

Summary.   The above discussion has suggested ways in which each type of experience might be used most effectively. In the chart shown above, an attempt has been made to summarize the previous two sections by identifying those ways in which the various experiences might contribute to the 10 objectives listed earlier. Research to establish these relationships is virtually nonexistent. Informal studies are often made of student opinion. The chart presents a subjective projection based upon experience, but one which may serve two primary purposes. It can be used as a guide by those who are designing professional courses and direct experiences, and perhaps it may stimulate increased research in this important area. The headings at the top of the chart give the types of experience, while the headings on the side give the key words from the list of ten objectives given in full on pages 23–24.

A Theoretical Approach

Even a perfunctory review of the literature on student teaching in the last 75 years leads quickly to the conclusion that there is no comprehensive theoretical rationale for the contributions of student teaching and related direct experiences to the development of a professional teacher. The frequent recurrence of the same proposals, problems, and practices is most distressing for it clearly demonstrates the lack of a clear rationale, an unfamiliarity with the historical development, and a failure by many to profit from the successes and mistakes of others. Not infrequently at the Association for Student Teaching meetings one hears a person, who is returning to this field after an absence of some years, say, "This sounds just like where I came in before. They are talking about the same problems and proposing the same solutions!"

The writings on student teaching and teacher education of the first third of this century have a very different approach and character from those which have appeared since, and if read by some of the harshest critics of the present, might help them to see the great progress that has been made. Purposes of student teaching were frequently listed, but much of the approach was of a mechanistic sort built in large part on detailed job analyses of the teachers' work and of student teachers' activities, and taught through practice that resembled apprentice training. Teacher shortages, inadequate college budgets, lack of facilities for student teaching, poor salaries —all these problems of a bygone era have a familiar ring. But one article stood out then as now—probably the most penetrating

theoretical analysis of student teaching yet written—John Dewey's
essay on "The Relation of Theory to Practice in Education."[7] Presented in 1904 to the National Society for the Scientific Study of
Education, Dewey differentiates clearly between experience for the
development of skill and that for supporting the learning of theory.
In the later portions of the essay he develops chronologically a suggested progression of emphases in student teaching, which forms a
sound basis for much of the "cookbook" type of writing for supervising teachers today, and he has much to say to those who have
designed some of the innovations of recent years.[8] The three excerpts which follow develop the main theme of the essay:

> On one hand, we may carry on the practical work with the object
> of giving teachers in training command of the necessary tools of
> their profession; control of the technique of class instruction and
> management; skill and proficiency in the work of teaching. With
> this aim in view, practice work is, as far as it goes, of the nature of
> apprenticeship. On the other hand, we may propose to use practice
> work as an instrument in making real and vital theoretical instruc-
> tion; the knowledge of subject matter and of principles of educa-
> tion. This is the laboratory point of view.[9]
>
> Practice work thus considered is administered primarily with
> reference to the intellectual reactions it incites, giving the student
> a better hold upon the educational significance of the subject-matter
> he is acquiring, and of the science, philosophy, and history of edu-
> cation. Of course, the *results* are not exclusive. It would be very
> strange if practice work in doing what the laboratory does for a
> student of physics or chemistry in way of securing a more vital
> understanding of its principles, should not at the same time insure
> some skill in the instruction and management of a class.[10]
>
> Nonetheless, there is a fundamental difference in the conception
> and conduct of the practice work according as one idea or the other
> is dominant and the other subordinate. If the primary object of
> practice is acquiring skill in performing the duties of a teacher, then

[7] John Dewey, "The Relation of Theory to Practice in Education," in *The Third Yearbook of the National Society for the Scientific Study of Education,* ed. Charles A. McMurry (Bloomington, Illinois: Public School Publishing Company, 1904). Reprinted by the Association for Student Teaching as *Bulletin No. 17* (Cedar Falls, Iowa: The Association, 1962).

[8] *Ibid.,* pp. 26–29.
[9] *Ibid.,* p. 9.
[10] *Ibid.,* p. 10.

the amount of time given to practice work, the place at which it is introduced, the method of conducting it, of supervising, criticizing, and correlating it, will differ widely from the method where the laboratory ideal prevails; and *vice versa*.[11]

---

[11] *Ibid.*, p. 10.

CHAPTER III

Patterns of Organization
for Student Teaching

Traditionally the authority and responsibility for public education in America has been left to the states and the local districts, while teacher education, as a function of both publicly-supported and private colleges and universities, has enjoyed even more freedom to develop in diverse ways. But as state certification requirements became more comprehensive, states have increased their leadership and responsibility over many aspects of teacher education. Nevertheless there are few areas of American education today in which there is greater variety, more unusual adaptations, and more confusion, with fewer clear-cut trends than in the student-teaching phases of teacher education. Certainly few educators or critics from the lay public would insist upon rigid uniformity, but the present chaotic situation dissipates most unwisely the resources of institutions and the energies of many professional people.

Both the critics and the would-be-reformers would be on much more solid ground if there were detailed, comprehensive analyses of the practices, purposes, and problems of student teaching, and the success of the product of present programs. The Flowers Report[1] surveyed in depth the teachers colleges and a sampling of private liberal arts colleges, but since that time the major studies reported have been much more limited in scope. In 1952, Rucker reported trends from 1932;[2] in 1959, Woodruff surveyed the member institutions of the American Association of Colleges for Teacher

---

[1] Sub-Committee of the Standards and Surveys Committee, *School and Community Laboratory Experiences in Teacher Education* (Oneonta, N.Y.: American Association of Teachers Colleges, 1948).

[2] W. Ray Rucker, "Trends in Student Teaching—1932 to 1952," *The Journal of Teacher Education*, IV, No. 4 (1953), 261–263.

Education,[3] while this organization reported a 1961 study of 121 Liberal Arts Colleges;[4] and in 1963, Nelson reported on student teaching in the eight southeastern states.[5] Many less comprehensive studies have appeared including those done for the various yearbooks of the Association for Student Teaching, especially the 1951, 1954, and 1961 volumes, but much searching is necessary to get a reasonably comprehensive picture of the development, status, and wide ramifications of student teaching and related experiences. This chapter presents an overview of practice and some of the problem areas in student teaching.

Developmental Periods

In the century and a quarter of its history, the development of student teaching appears to have been greatly affected by a succession of powerful influences. This writer finds that charting some of these *major influences* helps in interpreting present conditions and problems and in plotting a course for the future.

Personal and institutional forces, 1837 to 1920. The origin and early development of student teaching was the product of the creative minds of some distinguished educators and the institutions they established. After the Civil War the enrollment in both elementary and secondary schools increased steadily with a concurrent demand for teachers; and the idea of professional education for all types of teachers slowly gained general acceptance. Both certification and training was largely local, and except for an occasional committee report there were few national or state agencies or organizations pressing for practical experiences for prospective teachers.

Official agencies and organizations, 1920 to 1950. During this period, as the authority for secondary school teacher certification was consolidated in state departments, student teaching was prac-

---

[3] Asahel D. Woodruff, *Student Teaching Today,* AACTE Study Series, Number 5 (Washington, D.C.: The American Association of Colleges for Teacher Education, 1960).

[4] Subcommittee on Teacher Education in Liberal Arts Colleges of the Committee on Studies, *Liberal Arts Colleges and Teacher Education,* AACTE Study Series, Number 7 (Washington, D.C.: The American Association of Colleges for Teacher Education, 1963), pp. 23–34.

[5] Horace Nelson, "A Study of Student Teaching Practices in Eight Southeastern States," *The Journal of Teacher Education,* XIV, No. 2 (1963), 188–193.

tically legislated into college curricula. Some states also developed standards for teacher-education programs and began the practice of approving institutions for the preparation of teachers of specific subjects and levels. The American Association of Teachers Colleges adopted standards for evaluating its member institutions at this same time; the practice evolved into accreditation, but was limited at first to teachers colleges. With the Smith-Hughes Act of 1917 the federal government began subsidizing teacher education in home economics and agriculture, with later laws broadening the base for teacher education in other vocational fields.

Public schools since 1950. In the post-war period many forces were at work, but the critical need of the public schools for new staff and the demands of the colleges for more and more teacher-education laboratories in the public schools were the dominant forces. As the colleges braced themselves for the tidal wave of students and struggled to find resources, it was not surprising for some college presidents to suggest that public schools take over completely the supervision of student teachers. Fifth-year programs with their apprentice-type beginners also put new and large demands upon the administrative and supervisory services of the schools. As the number of student teachers increased, classroom teacher groups and state teacher associations began to take note of the chaotic patterns of assignment, requirements, and compensation, and sought ways to bring colleges and schools together to work out problems.

With the new standards for professional laboratory experiences growing out of the 1948 Flowers Report, many colleges tried to improve and expand their programs only to be frustrated by added costs and rising numbers. In 1954 the accreditation function was taken over by the National Council on Accreditation in Teacher Education (NCATE), and Standard VI on professional laboratory experiences and student teaching was gradually rewritten in more quantitative and less threatening form than the original proposal in the Flowers Report. The Association for Student Teaching (AST) has always had an influence out of all proportion to its size. Before the 1950's, it had no more than 500 members, but it produced a major part of the literature in this field and had on its rolls most of the nationally known leaders in student teaching. After World War

II, most of the AST members were from college and laboratory school faculties, but as student teaching moved out into the public schools, the members were recruited from public school faculties as well, and its membership grew to around 4000, including many state units.

College administrators and staff struggled with their problems, but usually found themselves dealing with emergencies and minor problems, unable to stop long enough to make a thorough study and attack upon the major issues. College personnel, from instructors to top administrators, now began to sense that any real improvement in student teaching had to be a joint effort with the public schools.

Future forces? State and national support and regulation?   In 1949 when Haskew first proposed state responsibility,[6] few people had even considered, much less advocated, assigning the state the responsibility for providing high quality teacher-education laboratories for all colleges, both public and private. Many of the leaders in the field have come to believe that state programs are the only way to provide some order and adequate financial support for student teaching. Following his two year study of teacher education Conant devoted his fourth recommendation to this point.

> The state should provide financial assistance to local boards to insure high-quality practice teaching as part of the preparation of teachers enrolled in either private or public institutions.[7]

National accreditation by NCATE, while still somewhat on trial, is an actuality. The National Education Association (NEA) through its Commission on Teacher Education and Professional Standards (TEPS) has outlined an expanded program of professional laboratory experiences as a part of its comprehensive "New Horizons" approach to the improvement of the profession.[8] More recently TEPS

---

[6] L. D. Haskew, "Framework for Student Teaching: A Proposal." *Education,* LXX, No. 2 (1949), 152.

[7] James B. Conant, *The Education of American Teachers* (New York: McGraw-Hill Book Company, 1963), p. 64.

[8] National Commission on Teacher Education and Professional Standards, *New Horizons for the Teaching Profession,* ed. Margaret Lindsey (Washington, D.C.: National Education Association, 1961).

has emphasized the state approach to student teaching in its *Position Paper*.[9]

Several states have study groups at work on comprehensive state plans providing for state responsibility both through regulation and state support. With all the discussion and controversy over federal aid to education, it is hardly surprising that some are beginning to raise the question of possible federal support for teacher education. If the Congress were to make matching grants to those states which develop state programs for subsidizing all school systems and personnel serving teacher-education functions, the colleges could put their resources into improving their campus programs. Supporting teacher education in this way might very well prove to be one of the best ways to support and improve education generally.

Types of Laboratory Facilities

The first laboratory schools used for student teaching appear to have been special schools established by the colleges. Well before the early 1900's a wide variety of arrangements developed, in addition to these essentially private "practice" schools, ranging from the use of regular public schools by agreement to college controlled off-campus laboratory schools. Sometimes the administrator of the laboratory school was principal or superintendent of the school and professor or director of student teaching on the faculty; sometimes the faculty were selected and paid by both school and college, and colleges often furnished the buildings and supplies as well as contributing to the total operating budget. Armentrout wrote one of the best historical accounts of these institutions and also described many of the arrangements for laboratory schools at State Teachers Colleges in the 1920's.[10]

Probably most such arrangements up to that time had been agreements worked out personally by the people involved and without

---

9 National Commission on Teacher Education and Professional Standards, *A Position Paper* (Washington, D.C.: National Education Association, 1963).

10 Winfield D. Armentrout, *The Conduct of Student Teaching in State Teachers Colleges* (Greeley, Colo.: Colorado State Teachers College, 1927), pp. 1–12, 165–172.

any legal sanction, for Armentrout reports a law suit in Iowa in which a district court held "that the school board had abused its discretion in making arrangements with the Iowa State Teachers College for student teaching in the schools of the district.[11] The finding, however, was later reversed by the State Supreme Court. Cases such as this may very well have prompted the passage in several mid-west states of enabling legislation for the construction and operation of laboratory schools under joint school-college sponsorship.

Even though many of these teachers colleges were relatively small, they were faced with real problems in the concentration of college students in their laboratory schools. Armentrout reports a sampling of colleges in which the ratio of college students to pupils in the campus schools ranged from one student to .27 pupils up to one student to .54 pupils, while in the college controlled public schools the ratios ranged from one student to 1.2 pupils to one student to 3.5 pupils.[12] Under such conditions the number of student teachers per supervising teacher was found in various studies to range from one to 50 at any given time with the medians being four, six, eight, 14; and the medians ran as high as 29 student teachers per teacher during a school year. Consequently the 1928 version of the standards of the American Association of Teachers Colleges (AATC) set 18 students per year as the maximum to be supervised by one training school teacher; and the Carnegie standards recommended eight as a desirable number at one time. Similarly the AATC recommended that the regular teachers do two-fifths of the teaching in the laboratory school, while the Carnegie standards recommended one-half of the teaching time and never less than one-fourth.[13]

With loads such as that in the on- and off-campus laboratory schools, the transfer of the locale for student teaching to the public schools following World War II proved to be a major shift because only one, or at most two, student teachers were placed with any one public school teacher, and often only one per year. Some universities and many liberal arts colleges already had good working

---

[11] *Ibid.*, p. 165.
[12] *Ibid.*, p. 159.
[13] *Ibid.*, pp. 155–157.

arrangements with public schools, but even these facilities have often been overtaxed by the increasing enrollments. Two factors are critical—the total number of student teachers to be served in a given locality from all colleges, and the number of available experienced teachers from whom to choose. Since many colleges and universities are located in relatively small communities, the rising numbers of student teachers forced colleges to move their operations outside the local commuting area. The range of facilities now being used as student-teaching laboratories can be summarized as follows:

1. Campus laboratory school or schools;
2. Off-campus laboratory school or schools;
3. Off-campus public schools in the local area;
4. Off-campus public schools at some distance;
5. Off-campus centers, usually at some distance;
6. Some combination of two or more of the above.

At present campus laboratory schools receive few student teachers except for preliminary experiences or as special cases, while off-campus laboratory schools with some real college control are becoming much less frequent. Outside of metropolitan areas few colleges of any size can find adequate facilities for their student teachers without going some distance from the campus, and probably a majority actually use a combination of types. Many of the larger institutions use schools 100 to 200 miles away, and some students, even in the eastern states, travel 300 and 400 miles, while those in the mountain states may go as far as 700 miles from the campus.

With distances such as these, changes are inevitable in student-teaching programs and sometimes even in the curriculum. One of the first institutions to develop the concept of a formal student-teaching center was Michigan State University, and now many others are adopting this pattern because it does offer solutions to several problems. The local coordinator can follow through on administrative matters, work at public relations, visit and supervise the student teachers, hold regular seminars to substitute for the ones formerly held on campus, carry on an in-service program for the supervising teachers, and on occasions teach a course to the student teachers. Sometimes campus staff go out and live in a center, while others commute, but many colleges are hiring persons resident in the community for this particular service, including some retired school personnel.

The fifth-year programs, including many supported by the Fund for the Advancement of Education, have brought another dimension into the problem of finding adequate student-teaching stations, that of arranging for the employment of full- or part-time apprentices and interns. Directors of student teaching report that a given school system can absorb a much smaller number of employed apprentice-interns than regular student teachers. It also appears probable that the number of teachers qualified and interested in serving as intern supervisors is much less than those able and willing to receive student teachers.

From the published reports one can infer that most of the students in these subsidized and demonstration fifth-year programs come from middle and upper socio-economic levels and are often employed as apprentice-interns in suburban areas and small cities where many of them continue to teach. By contrast, teacher shortages are most acute in the less favored portions of large cities and in the more rural areas, while school administrators from both these types of districts are usually more successful in recruiting graduates of regular four-year programs. Any major shift in the teacher-education curriculum or in the proportion of teachers prepared by the various types, such as a move to fifth-year programs or to a required five-year plan with internship, could seriously affect the supply of new teachers available to certain areas and types of communities.

Competition among colleges for student-teaching stations is already becoming acute in many areas, and will step up decidedly as more cities take action such as that taken in Charlotte, North Carolina to limit the 12 colleges using the schools there, to a total of 400 student teacher placements per year. But college enrollments continue to rise and in 1962–63 there were 14 per cent more secondary school student teachers in the country than the previous year. To try to cope with this problem some cities, such as Philadelphia and Los Angeles, have developed bulletins of regulations and procedures as a guide for college faculties and students working there. Some years ago a cooperative approach among 33 colleges and the New York City School system resulted in a very excellent set of guides for all types of personnel involved in student teaching.[14]

Only two other approaches, thus far tried, seem to offer much promise for improving the quality of experiences and at the same time solving some of these problems of overuse of schools and competition among colleges for places. First, the states can set up comprehensive plans through the state department of education to take over the responsibility for providing good quality laboratories through regulation, compensation, and a coordinated effort at in-service education of needed personnel. With or without a state program some metropolitan areas will be forced to find some machinery for enlisting the support of both colleges and public schools in developing policy, setting minimum standards of practice, and coordinating the operation. Second, a few local teacher-education councils have been formed, and this appears the most likely device to cope with the problems in a given city or other local area.

Nature of Assignments

Early in this century student teachers regularly spent an hour or a period a day in a school room concentrating on instruction. By contrast, in the earlier period the assignments seem to have been more varied, with a common pattern similar to many of the fifth-year apprenticeship plans of the present, in which one master teacher moved among two, four or even eight students who had complete charge of the actual instruction. After completion of student teaching, most students say that their experience was too short; and this criticism added to several others has fostered the trend toward larger and larger blocks of time for student teaching. Among the arguments influencing the increases were the desire to have the student become more actively involved in the school and its community, and to experience as nearly as possible all the roles of the teacher.

Although in general the trend continues for longer student-teach-

[14] Board of Education of the City of New York, *Student Teaching in the Elementary Schools* (New York: Board of Education of the City of New York, n.d.)

ing assignments, the most powerful influence has not been educational but rather one of geography. When colleges place student teachers more than 25 miles from the campus, full-time temporary residence in the school community becomes almost a necessity. For many years faculties of home economics and agriculture have insisted upon their student teachers living in the school community, and many other subject fields advocate this practice vigorously.

Full-time assignments provide numerous advantages, including an opportunity to concentrate on this important experience without the distractions of campus activities. But many student and administrative problems must be solved. Often seniors are heavily involved in campus leadership roles and in such activities as athletics and dramatics which must either be dropped or fitted into the student teaching schedule. Finding good living quarters for students in off-campus centers is often difficult and an added expense to the student, while the college has to adjust to the mass exodus from dormitories and therefore a reduction of income. Many college students are married and have children, and thus when one member of a couple is scheduled away from the campus this presents problems and requests for special consideration. Early decisions on assignments are a necessity, and administering a large off-campus student-teaching program has become a very complex and difficult scheduling and placement operation.

In shifting to full-time assignments, from those of one hour a day for a semester or more, college adminstrators have tried a great number of plans which varied in length from two weeks to a full semester. Some colleges even excused students for a two to six week full-time assignment within a regular semester thus penalizing the student both by too brief a student-teaching experience and too much absence from other courses. Various kinds of schedules have been devised, many of them called *block plans,* as a part of a professional semester of concentrated professional study. A very desirable application of this plan, from an educational point of view, provides a few weeks of concentrated professional courses on campus, a somewhat larger block of weeks in student teaching and a shorter follow-up or evaluation period back on campus. Some common examples include an 18-week semester divided into three blocks of weeks such as 7-9-2, 6-6-6, or 5-12-1, with the first number in each case being the weeks on campus, the second that of student teaching, and the third back on campus.

Increasing numbers of students and the problem of maintaining a high rate of occupancy in self-liquidating dormitories are forcing some institutions to arbitrary plans which pit the off-campus student teachers against a campus group taking short term courses, usually of a professional nature. For example, group A may be off-campus while group B is taking the courses *prior* to student teaching, and then at mid-semester time the groups shift so that group B is off-campus while group A is studying the same block of courses *following* their student teaching. Any desired uniformity of sequence of courses is lost thereby, but perhaps careful observers will be able to learn which pattern gives the best results.

Recent studies indicate that there are about as many half-time student teaching plans as full-time, with a much smaller percentage remaining on a one or two period or hour a day basis. Most students assigned on the half-day basis are placed on or near the campus or within easy commuting distance so that they can return for other classes. Usually public transportation facilities are totally inadequate. Many of these commuters either travel in private car pools or have transportation arranged by the college. Some colleges are avoiding the dangers of travel liability, either by furnishing the transportation or by arranging blanket liability insurance policies covering all student driven cars. Student teaching has always been a relatively expensive course, but all types of costs are rising. Liberal Arts Colleges especially, but also colleges of all types, often pass these costs on to the student by charging high student-teaching fees from which they pay such charges as remuneration to cooperating schools, transportation and expenses of college supervisors, and sometimes even student transportation.

Course credit earned through student teaching is another area of extreme variation. Early standards by the American Association of Teachers Colleges fixed five semester hours of credit as the amount to be earned by a one hour a day assignment for a semester (a total of 90 periods or hours) during which the student taught about two-thirds of the time or 60 hours. State certification requirements have varied in recent years from two to 15 semester hours of credit with five or six semester hours being the common minimum, and requirements for elementary school teachers often being higher than for secondary school teachers. Some states stipulate a certain minimum number of clock hours of teaching and observation while others set standards only in credit hours, suggesting or requiring some ratio of clock hours to credit hours. The use of clock hours of class instruction as the chief or sole criterion for credit and certification often leads to serious abuses. Almost inevitably students concentrate on getting hours completed to the exclusion of other desirable goals, and are ready to take their leave when they reach the minimum number.

Recently many colleges have been considering calendar changes. It is too early to estimate the effect of the trimester on student teaching except to observe that the third or spring trimester (sometimes called summer trimester) will include only a small number of weeks that overlap the public school calendar before the end of the school year. In many ways the quarter system has advantages because it provides three assignment periods. A full-time assignment for a quarter gives 15 quarter hours of credit, or only 10 semester hours, out of the total hours allowed for professional courses. Under the semester plan a student assigned full-time for the entire term earns 15 semester hours which preempts a large fraction of the professional credit block. At the secondary level the winter quarter has real disadvantages because it extends across the semester break in the schools. Teachers are reluctant to let students start teaching until after review and semester examinations are over and the new semester begins. This leaves a very brief period for teaching.

The desirable length of assignment is related directly to the rate of maturation during student teaching. Some of the most experienced leaders in this field believe that nine weeks is the shortest total time in which to expect the average student to mature desirably even with a long and well-planned program of pre-student-teaching experiences. In his personal prescription for student teaching, Conant describes the desired details at the elementary school level as a part of his eighteenth recommendation:

> All future elementary teachers should engage in practice teaching for a period of at least 8 weeks, spending a minimum of 3 hours a day in the classroom; the period must include at least 3 weeks of full responsibility for the classroom under the direction of

a cooperating teacher and the supervision of a clinical professor.

The amount of practice teaching I am prescribing would carry 8 semester hours of credit.[15]

The trend and general opinion would probably favor not less than nine weeks of full-time student teaching as a minimum with a longer assignment desirable for students who had made only limited professional growth. But again, a major reorganization of professional courses in teacher education might very well produce a shift in the objectives of student teaching that would result in a different basic pattern.

Curriculum Provisions

Prior to 1930 most student teaching, as well as observation and participation, was organized and offered as discrete courses and included all the direct experiences for the entire professional curriculum. The idea of a planned sequence of experiences appears to have evolved largely between 1930 and 1950 when different experiences were made an integral part of given courses at many colleges. As more thought was given to the sequence of professional courses and experiences, faculties began to search for ways to make learning more functional. One common approach was to combine courses and experiences into large blocks, and this led to the development of professional semesters and quarters—sometimes excluding student teaching, but later often including it in the so-called block approach as described in the last section.

Another proposal sometimes tried was to offer student teaching earlier in the curriculum so that students could have more professional courses and post-student-teaching experiences afterwards. In recent years faculties often have found themselves unable to make this change because of the popular pressure to increase content in the subject areas and to require the completion of most of these courses before student teaching. A very few institutions offer two sessions of student teaching, sometimes one rather early in the college career and another near the end, but more often one following the other directly in the senior year or in the late junior and early senior years.

---

[15] James B. Conant, *The Education of American Teachers* (New York: McGraw-Hill Book Company, 1963), p. 162.

Many different adaptations have been devised and explored in an effort to improve student teaching. Originally the September Field Experience had been designed primarily for beginning sophomores, but increasing numbers of colleges are sending student teachers to their assigned schools in September prior to the opening of the colleges. This practice extends the student teaching to an important part of the school year which students often do not see otherwise; and when possible, both first and second semester student teachers have a full-time September experience together.

Originally, at many institutions, the weekly group seminar for student teachers was much like any other course, including topics and assignments such as might be found in general methods courses. The trend has been toward organizing smaller seminars where content grows more directly out of the student-teaching experiences and thus becomes more functional. Unless off-campus student-teaching at a distance is organized on some more or less formal center basis, the group seminar is largely lost and with it the possibilities for a functional and intellectual analysis and evaluation of the experience. Most public school teachers find it very difficult to achieve in their conferences with one student teacher the educational values of the group seminar.

The serious and continuing teacher shortage since World War II has brought many problems to teacher-education institutions as well as to the schools and school administrators. The many emergency programs have seriously dissipated the energies and facilities of the colleges, and brought with them several continuing demands for meeting new emergencies and for solving many very complex professional problems of individual teachers. Thousands of individuals have entered teaching on emergency certificates before completing planned preparatory programs and indeed too often with no professional study. Many of these teachers continue taking part-time and summer courses and finally meet all certification requirements except for student teaching. Obviously, any enrollment in student teaching by an experienced in-service teacher would not be student teaching by the very nature of the case.

Probably the most common arrangement to meet this problem has been to require these teachers to enter a college in the summer and to enroll in a modified type of student teaching offered in a campus school or some other special summer school. The emphasis varies greatly in different institutions but some of the most defensible objectives would be to provide an opportunity for the teacher to study a greater variety of learning activities; to receive some professional evaluation of his teaching; to have experienced college faculty judge his adequacy for full certification and recommendation for a degree, if that is involved; and to have filed with his credentials in the placement office an evaluation of his performance. Unfortunately many colleges do not have any summer schools available for this purpose and a few institutions have arranged for these non-certificated teachers to enroll for a minimum of credit under a student teaching plan and have a *supervised teaching experience—not a student-teaching experience*—while in-service. Carefully designed, this program can render a real professional service provided, of course, that the distance does not cause the supervision to be too costly in time and travel.

Two critical issues can arise, however, in handling these special cases. If the school principal is most appreciative of the teacher's efforts because he is filling a vacancy, and if the college supervisor considers the quality of teaching so low as not to warrant a satisfactory evaluation, then a sticky professional and sometimes ethical problem arises which is hard to resolve. Some colleges will only agree to give college credit for this enrollment in supervised in-service teaching when the teacher arranges to go on a part-time employed status, thus permitting a significant fraction of each teaching day to be considered student status, without pay. Taking such a reduction in salary is strenuously resisted by many, and is especially difficult for heads of families.

The literature includes frequent mention of team teaching and the use of the new media, including teaching machines. Many observers question whether the team teaching concept has been as well developed, both theoretically and practically, as it should be, and, therefore, whether many school faculties are really ready to introduce student teachers into their teams except as observer-participants, rather than as full student teachers working as part of a team. The concept of team teaching is a very old one, for laboratory school teachers both on- and off-campus were often very skillful in developing a team relationship with groups of student teachers (actually only the term and its present connotation is new).

But schools differ sharply in their use and approach to team teaching just as they do in the adequacy of their equipment and their use of the various new media, especially teaching machines. How much should student teachers' experiences be confined to these new approaches? Should all student teachers be introduced to these devices? These are curricular questions which every college will answer directly or by default. And no matter how the faculty wants to answer these and many more questions implied in this and other chapters, the availability of good schools and a sufficient number of supervising teachers will have all too much to do with the curricular decisions which will finally be made in regard to student teaching.

The "Team" in Student Teaching

Persons who have been working with student teachers in recent years, no longer have any illusions that student-teaching programs to be effective, must be real team or joint operations between schools and colleges. Both the colleges and the public schools are deeply involved in teacher education, and although the balance of responsibility may shift as the organization and emphasis shifts, both institutions will continue to be involved. Current literature clearly reflects the growing recognition of the important role of the public schools and especially of the ever increasing range of types of personnel in both public schools and colleges who have a major contribution to make to the student-teaching program.

The accompanying diagrammatic listing was prepared to show graphically that there are two "teams" responsible for student teaching, and that a close coordination of the efforts of the two teams is essential to produce a high quality program. All the major types of personnel are listed in the two separate lines of authority, and there can be no crossing of this authority. The student teacher is moved physically out of the college line and placed into the school line, but only to receive delegated responsibility and not final authority. Each major position on each side has a correlative position on the other side, even though in small schools and colleges some of these types of positions would not appear.

THE "TEAM" RESPONSIBLE FOR STUDENT TEACHING

THE COLLEGE TEAM   THE PUBLIC SCHOOL TEAM

Responsible for Policy Action

Board of Trustees   Board of Education
President   Superintendent of Schools

Responsible for Policy Development

| Local Teacher Education Council |
| (Advisory and Mutual Consent) |

Dean   * * * *   Superintendent or Assistant
                                                       Superintendent

Student Teaching Council   Advisory Council
  (or Committee)   (or Committee)

Director or Coordinator of   * * * *   Coordinator of Teacher
  Laboratory Experiences   Education Services

Department Chairman   Principal

Staff Personnel   Staff Personnel

Responsible for Operation

Director of Student Teaching   * * * *   Principal

Coordinator of Student Teaching   Coordinator of Student
  Center (or Curriculum Area)   Teaching (in a School)

Responsible for Immediate Supervision

College Supervisor   * * * *   Cooperating Teacher

| Student Teacher | | Student Teacher |

                                                        Pupils

Note: The student teacher acquires his status in the College Team, but by agreement is permitted to carry delegated responsibilities within the Public School Team.
   Many situations will be much simpler than those diagrammed, but the essential personnel in any given case should be easily identifiable. Several of the natural and proper channels of communication between correlative positions are indicated thus, * * * *.

It is most unfortunate that many of the persons working in student teaching have never had any direction in thinking through these relationships. Furthermore, only a very few of the positions have had their roles in student teaching carefully delineated in the literature—much having been written about the cooperating teacher, an increasing amount about the college supervisor, a little about the principal, and an occasional brief mention about the rest. Student teachers are urged to get acquainted with the specialists and their functions in the public schools, but the supporting role of similar staff persons in the colleges, who serve as consultants and specialists, is seldom mentioned. Much study, analysis, and research is needed to aid this complex professional team in improving their operations.

Regardless of how much responsibility the public schools assume, the college and its faculty are still the focal point for improvement in teacher education, because they must exercise the leadership and develop the principles to undergird the practice and provide much of the training for all levels of personnel. As the colleges have expanded their off-campus programs the problems encountered have been many and difficult. In 1959 Davies made a survey of the problems encountered by AACTE institutions during the establishment of their off-campus student teaching after the early stages of its operation. Only about half of the institutions which replied had such programs. He categorized the problems in six clusters under these headings:

1. Identification, recruitment, training, and compensation of supervising teachers
2. Recruitment, training, and compensation of college supervisors
3. Student personnel problems and services
4. Curricular and extra-curricular adjustments on campus
5. The determination of the length of student teaching assignments and credit allocation
6. Inter-college relationships[16]

This chapter has given emphasis to items 4 and 5 with some mention of 3 and 6. The following chapters will include some concern for items 1 and 2 especially.

Summary

In an earlier study of off-campus student teaching in the 1951 Yearbook of the Association for Student Teaching, Herrick makes

[16] Don Davies, "A Survey of College Problems and Practices in Off-Campus Student Teaching Programs," *Teacher Education and the Public Schools,* Fortieth Yearbook (Cedar Falls, Iowa: The Association for Student Teaching, 1961), p. 147.

his concluding generalization in this way, "The educational, administrative, and financial relationships and responsibilities of the teacher training institution and the cooperating school systems are variable, complex, important, and frequently muddled."[17] Real progress has taken place in student teaching when viewed over the long period of years, but, unfortunately, the above quotation must still be considered accurate. No reorganization in and of itself is going to improve teacher education and student teaching fundamentally. Good organizational structure based on sound theory could and should release the creative energy of able people to evolve an improved program in teacher education.

17 Virgil E. Herrick, "The Future of Off-Campus Programs," *Off-Campus Student Teaching*, Thirtieth Yearbook (Cedar Falls, Iowa: The Association for Student Teaching, 1951), p. 124.

CHAPTER IV

Responsibility for the Supervision
of Student Teaching

The crucial issues in the supervision of student teachers are (1) who will direct the work of student teachers, and (2) how skillfully will it be done. There are professional artist teachers whose student teachers enthusiastically express their appreciation for the wise counsel and sensitive effective direction they have received. On the other hand, unfortunately, there are teachers who could scarcely make the student-teaching experience any worse if they had studiously set out to do so.

The teachers now working with student teachers number in the hundreds of thousands, and a relatively small percentage have had extensive leadership in thinking through their role or formal training for it. Any major change in student teaching will be greatly affected by the adequacy of the classroom supervision or the lack of it. There is a growing group of teacher educators who believe that either the colleges must find a way and the necessary support to improve the quality of student teaching or that the responsibility will be turned over to other agencies.

This chapter is an attempt to analyze these issues. Since it is impossible to treat all the important and perplexing aspects of the supervision of student teachers, any real discussion of some have been deliberately omitted, such as the evaluation of student teachers and the relation of guidance theory to supervision. The importance of this latter point is emphasized by Burkhart, who makes this disturbing but very pertinent observation:

> Thus, this paradox exists: the individual most likely to have training as a specialist in guidance has the least opportunity to find

and correct (difficulties faced by student teachers), whereas the person least likely to be trained as a specialist (in guidance) has the best opportunity to detect such difficulties.[1]

Dual Supervision—A Professional Approach

In general, the quality of the supervision of student teaching dropped markedly and its character changed radically with the shift in locus and personnel from laboratory schools to public schools. Naturally this result was not universal, for there have long been and still are many very competent cooperating public school teachers. The problem, however, was sharply accentuated by the rapidity of the shift after World War II with no time for "tooling up" new personnel to new responsibilities. With the exploding college population there has been no respite.

The effect of the shift can be pointed up sharply by an analysis of the two traditional types of organization for supervision and a slowly emerging third type which is probably ideal for the present undergraduate. Historically, the first common pattern was the *laboratory-school* type. After the beginning of this century another form developed at colleges which were using public schools for student teaching. This second type can be described as the *college-controlled public school* pattern. Neither of these appears often in their original, or extreme, form, but both are in rather sharp contrast to the third which may be classified as the *dual responsibility* or *professional* type. Seldom does an analysis and comparison of these types appear in the literature.[2]

Laboratory school type. The director of student teaching made the placements, conducted the weekly group conference, kept the records, observed very occasionally, helped with the problem cases, and transmitted the grades to the registrar. Perhaps he carried as much as 10 per cent of the total supervisory responsibility, and his normal load would be 100 or more student teachers.

---

[1] Russell Burkhart, "Guidance Emphases in Student Teaching," *Guidance in Teacher Education*, Thirty-Sixth Yearbook (Cedar Falls, Iowa: The Association for Student Teaching, 1957), p. 119.

[2] L. O. Andrews, "The Role of the College Supervisor of Student Teachers," *Supervising Student Teachers in Business Education*, NABTTI Bulletin 60 (Washington, D.C.: National Association of Business Teacher-Training Institutions, 1954), pp. 8–9.

The student teacher was assigned directly to the laboratory school teacher who carried all of the day-to-day responsibility for supervision except for infrequent consultation with the director. Carefully selected for this role and sometimes specifically prepared for it, this teacher often directed the entire experience of the student teacher, decided on his grade, and reported it to the director. Usually the laboratory school teacher carried 90 per cent or more of the responsibility for supervision. The normal load was from five to ten student teachers, but with numbers two and three times that not too uncommon. The success of this whole plan was dependent upon the competence of the laboratory school teacher, which was often very high.

College-controlled public school type. As originally conceived the placement was requested by the college and approved by the principal in proper fashion. But the college supervisor usually conducted the campus seminar, observed the student teacher each week followed by a personal conference, checked all lesson plans, was responsible for the over-all planning of instruction, and gave the final grade. He carried up to 90 per cent of the responsibility for supervision and his normal, full-time load was about 12 student teachers.

The public school teacher, on the other hand, merely gave the student teacher a place to teach. He was not required to help with the supervision, and too often did "just take his leave." Technically his only responsibility was to protect the rights of pupils, and he certainly was not required to carry more than 10 per cent of the supervisory load; but he often assumed far more responsibility out of a sense of professional obligation. He seldom had more than one student teacher in a year. Clearly the competence of the college supervisor was the key to the success of this plan. Many times they were old hands of long experience and much skill, but a succession of relatively untrained part-time graduate students of some teaching experience also filled these posts. Having a college staff member determining the content and teaching procedure in a public school often led to strained relations and sometimes to sharp controversy.

The evolving modifications of these patterns gave little promise of solving the problems inherent in the two plans—numbers in the first instance, quality and proper authority under the second.

Dual responsibility or *professional type.* Lying between the two types just described, the professional type is the logical focus toward which the other two have tended to shift. For its success it depends upon a sharing of professional responsibility among professionally trained and competent cooperating teachers and equally qualified college supervisors. Here the college supervisor would work primarily *through the classroom teacher,* meanwhile observing the student teacher a few times, holding follow-up conferences, running the campus seminar, and deciding on the final grade. He would carry from 20 to 40 per cent of the responsibility and a reasonable load could be from 20 to 35 student teachers depending on geographical distribution and the experience and competence of the cooperating teachers.

To be most effective, the cooperating teacher would have to be a superior classroom teacher, specifically prepared and demonstrably capable of guiding a student teacher most effectively. He would carry on all of the day-to-day planning and evaluating and most of the individual conferences. His teacher-education function would be recognized by a reduction in his regular duties. Desirably such a teacher could carry 80 per cent and certainly not less than 60 per cent of the responsibility, and would seldom have more than one student teacher at a time and not more than two a year. The total problem would seem capable of solution if there were enough such teachers. But there are not now and there are not likely to be for some years to come.

Two additional factors are developments of the last decade. Fifth-year certification programs with integral apprenticeships and internships are common, and they introduce a different type of supervisory responsibility. Various plans have been devised to free outstanding teachers for intern supervision, and most of them involve a reduced teaching load for the teacher-supervisor. If this type of program should become the normal pathway to certification before the teacher shortage ends, then the inadequate number of capable cooperating teachers would be even more critical than it is today.

Recently, however, a new concept is being advocated from several quarters, which in effect says that all supervision of student teachers and interns should be turned over to the public schools and that the colleges should return to their prime responsibilities of teaching content in general education and teaching subject areas, plus teaching a very limited amount of professional courses. Some college presidents have advocated the move strictly as an economy measure, and there are a few colleges, mostly liberal arts institutions, which are following this pattern. Those who are promoting the fifth-year apprenticeship plans do in effect delegate most of this responsibility to the schools. Thus Woodring in *New Directions in Teacher Education* gives the following as the sixth of his predictions for change in teacher education by 1970:

> It seems probable that responsibility for supervision for the intern will gradually pass from the college to the public schools. This change will occur for two reasons: a) supervision of the teaching of public school children by the college staff leads to a division of responsibility and to confusion on the part of the intern as to where his primary responsibility lies; b) supervisors from the college must spend too much of their time in travel and often are not available when most needed.[3]

On the other hand, Lieberman analyzes the problem on theoretical grounds, reasoning from an analysis of preparation for the several professions, thus:

> The growing trend in the professions generally to combine theoretical and practical training appears to have two major implications for education. First, there appears to be solid professional justification for the requirement of practice teaching. The second major implication of our discussion is that an exceedingly large number of practice teaching programs now in existence do not conform to well established principles of professional training. If practice teaching is to be a genuine professional internship, it should be taken under the supervision of those who give the theoretical training.[4]

It is worth noting that Lieberman is one of the keenest critics of student teaching as it is actually conducted, and thus his comments

---

[3] Paul Woodring, *New Directions in Teacher Education* (New York: The Fund for the Advancement of Education, 1957), p. 77.

[4] Myron Lieberman, *Education as a Profession* (Englewood Cliffs, N.J.: Prentice-Hall, Inc., 1956), p. 208.

suggest that the profession of teaching has some serious thinking to do in developing a sound rationale in student teaching.

The two quotations sharply accentuate the contrast between properly conceived *student teaching* and a truly professional *internship*. Reasoning by analogy from medical education, student teaching conforms to the third- and fourth-year clinical courses conducted by medical school professors, usually in university controlled hospitals. Internships, on the other hand, are provided by the profession at large in all kinds of hospitals, and there is much criticism today because interns receive so little teaching. In fact, as Lieberman points out, in some quarters there is sentiment in favor of abolishing the medical internship for its lack of contribution to the learning of the young doctor.[5]

In summary then, this author believes that both student teaching and a following internship can be properly designed to serve discretely different professional purposes, and that a defensible pattern of supervision for each can be organized and operated in an efficient and thoroughly professional manner. In the balance of this chapter the roles of the principal participants in the supervision of student teachers will be developed in an effort to describe a workable pattern of organization together with a comprehensive picture of the activities of the three major participants.

The Role of the Cooperating Teacher

Over the years, many have contended that any really competent teacher can be a good cooperating teacher, but long experience proves that for a surprising percentage of teachers this just isn't the case. Where once there was no literature to aid the teacher in learning how to do this professional task, now it is becoming reasonably adequate. But it simply isn't in the hands of those who need it. The most frequent question of a first-time, cooperating public school teacher is "What is expected of me?" Even without a knowledge of *how,* many understanding teachers could probably do rather well if they only knew exactly *what* to do and clearly understood the dimensions of a desirable relationship between cooperating teacher

[5] *Ibid.,* p. 209.

and student teacher. The following analysis of the function or role of the cooperating teacher is included in considerable detail for two reasons. First, the author is convinced that any teacher could improve his service to a student teacher by a serious attempt to follow this outline, and second, because this type of information does not appear in any brief statement in the literature. In addition, a thorough, theoretical analysis of this function is urgently needed, and the items in the following list could be backed up by concepts from the several disciplines. Many thousands of teachers ought to have extensive theoretical and practical preparation in this area, but unfortunately, the desperate need is for a higher level of performance, now.

This analysis is organized on a chronological basis to follow the student through the experience. The numbered items are areas of activity or functions for the most part, and the suggestions are made for a public school teacher away from the campus working under a college supervisor who comes to the school at least once every two or three weeks. For the sake of simplicity the term, student teacher, has been abbreviated to ST. Organizational patterns are so varied that this projection may not exactly fit local practice. But college or school administrators can easily make the needed adjustments since in most cases the function is the same—the only shift needed is in the person who will assume the responsibility. The last sentence at the end of several items gives suggestions especially appropriate for those teachers who are located far away from the college, or who are seldom visited by a college supervisor.

The role of the cooperating public school teacher

1. *Assignment.* Teacher given free choice, accepts ST in a situation at a time when circumstances are favorable and when extensive professional service can be given. Works with college supervisor before or soon after ST arrives to plan a well-balanced program of learning activities, asks college supervisor to designate the one teacher-advisor for each student, and to define exactly the part of the school day for which any other teacher will assume responsible direction.

2. *Acquaintance.* Gives cordial welcome as to a wanted associate; promotes easy, informal relations with self and other staff

members; arranges get-acquainted opportunity (out-of-school if possible) where sincere informality can take the place of the teacher-student relationship. When appropriate, assists ST in establishing residence, making adjustments to the community, and in getting a broader community orientation.

3. *Information exchange.* Secures from and shares with ST vital information, such as address, telephone number, schedule, and the like. Secures informal and formal record of ST's range of abilities, experiences, special skills and interests, and a usable summary of the college curriculum and philosophy. Shares his interests and specialties with ST.

4. *Orientation.* Provides ST with a place for his personal and professional materials, and provides areas at the school in which the ST may study, prepare materials, and work. Provides orientation to building, classes, school, faculty, the total staff team, school system, and community.

5. *Introduction of ST.* Prepares pupils for coming of ST. Makes friendly purposeful introduction of ST as a welcome new team member. Sets the stage for ST's initial successes and for pupils to regard ST as *The Teacher* when in charge of the class.

6. *Early observation.* Provides opportunity for observation of good teaching, of pupils, of course of study, all directed toward helping the ST get ready to teach. Demonstrates various procedures and methods to facilitate ST's growth in understanding and skill.

7. *Participation.* Encourages ST to participate in class by volunteering as a pupil with later reversal of roles. Assigns a succession of *routine* procedures. Arranges for ST to serve as his *assistant* in many teaching-learning activities. Helps ST prepare and carry through a series of increasingly difficult *bit teaching* activities (simple, unitary procedures) with individuals, small groups, and the full class.

8. *Joint evaluation.* Initially requests ST to evaluate cooperatively the teacher's own teaching with later reversal of roles. Arranges frequent conferences to evaluate progress of the teaching-learning with both practicing self-evaluation. When requested by the college, takes leadership in developing basic criteria on which success in student teaching will be judged.

9. *Initial teaching.* Assists ST in planning, and reviews detailed

planning with ST. Allows ST to take over full-teaching responsibility for stated periods followed by daily evaluation conferences during early stages.

10. *Delegated responsibilities.* Provides permissive atmosphere within professional limits by adjusting freedom and responsibility of ST to the ST's level of demonstrated competence. Arranges three-way conference (teacher, ST, and college supervisor) for clarification of roles and responsibilities. (The following chart suggests a division of responsibilities with areas which may be delegated to the ST.)

Area	Initial teaching	Sustained teaching	Major unit
Methods and activities	Teacher and ST	ST with teacher review	ST
Subject-matter content	Teacher	Teacher and ST	ST with teacher review
Curriculum and course design	School system and teacher	School system and teacher	Teacher and ST

11. *Planning procedure.* Directs ST in daily, long-range, and major unit planning in a format satisfactory to teacher and college supervisor, and in progressing from formal, detailed, written plans to a scheme ST can use satisfactorily in his on-the-job teaching. Assists ST in relating his planning to instructional emphases followed before ST arrived, and those to come later in the school year. Directs periodic joint evaluation of effectiveness of planning procedures.

12. *Instructional responsibility.* With ST, agrees on major emphases of instruction, units to be taught, and selection of ST's own major unit. Includes team planning and alternates instructional leadership throughout much of the assignment with both doing individual, small group, and class teaching. During ST's major unit has ST take over all aspects of directing learning including all related routines. If requested to do so, reports to college regularly on the activities of ST and his progress.

13. *Variety of activities.* Uses a variety of approaches himself and profits from ST's presence by exploring other approaches. Encourages ST to use variety, be creative in methodology, in solving teaching-learning problems, and in all the roles of the teacher, and

assists ST in appraisal of results. Aids ST in understanding applicability of school policies and the limits of professional freedom.

14. *Solving learning problems.* Gives ST freedom, encouragement, and assistance in attacking individual and group learning problems intensively and creatively. Supplies information and directs ST to other sources of data on pupils. Gives generous praise for observable progress with individual pupils.

15. *Classroom control—discipline.* Gives ST gradual induction into the pupil-control responsibilities of a teacher in keeping with the school climate and policies, and stands behind ST in all such matters. Recognizes that a teacher can delegate responsibilities but not final authority. (The following chart suggests a plan for a gradual shift of responsibilities to the student teacher as he demonstrates his competency.)

Responsibility	*Initial teaching*	*Sustained teaching*	*Major unit*
Managing the class	ST	ST	ST
Handling common behavior problems	Teacher	ST	ST
Handling major discipline cases	Teacher	Teacher	ST with teacher direction

16. *Pupil evaluation.* Familiarizes ST with school policies, procedures, and a variety of evaluation techniques. Arranges joint participation in evaluation and grading, but always reviews grades given by ST and assumes full responsibility.

17. *Noninstructional roles of teachers.* Arranges a planned series of observing, assisting, and full-responsibility roles for ST in many noninstructional activities with good breadth of contact and depth in some, including special duties of teachers, professional activities of the staff, and a wide variety of community-school relationships.

18. *Administrative and professional activities.* Shows ST the clerical and administrative responsibilities expected. Provides ST experience with the more common types of local routines and professional responsibilities. Aids ST in acquiring a wholesome attitude toward these obligations and helps ST find ways to do them quickly and accurately.

19. *Mid-term evaluation.* Arranges a carefully planned mid-term evaluation including ST's self-evaluation, teacher's semi-objective

evaluation, scheduled conference, plus three-way conference when possible and appropriate. Jointly identify objectives and desirable activities for balance of student teaching. When requested, completes formal mid-term evaluation and reports to the college.

20. *Promotion of ST growth.* Helps ST to learn to profit from self-evaluation of experience. Gives positive, nondominating suggestions. Supports ST in his efforts to overcome mistakes, to solve teaching, professional and related personal problems, and to seek help from qualified sources. Shares instruction, often at the request of the ST, with reversal of roles as an aid to ST learning. In the absence of a frequent college seminar, organizes a series of conferences on major areas of concern for this subject and grade level.

21. *Protecting the pupils.* Keeps constantly aware of the effectiveness of ST. Works closely with college supervisor and principal, keeping them informed of ST's progress and seeking their continued assistance and suggestions. Counsels with them when pupils' interests seem to be in jeopardy. Assumes major responsibility with the principal for requesting removal of ST when pupils are being harmed.

When a serious question arises as to the wisdom of allowing a ST to continue, the cooperating teacher informs both the college supervisor and principal at once. If the college supervisor does not immediately initiate a special evaluation, including conferences with teacher and principal at the school, the principal contacts the director or coordinator of student teaching. Action should be taken whenever all four (or three)—college director and supervisor plus teacher and principal—are convinced removal is the only sound professional course, or whenever either pair, at the school or at the college, are ready to recommend action and can document their reasons. The college staff should take the action and should hold a final conference with the student and with principal and teacher at the school. To allow time for professional study of critical situations, the teacher can take over the teaching while arranging for the ST to observe the teacher and others in the school.

22. *Later observation.* From the beginning of sustained teaching, directs ST in increasing amounts of observation of varied types of instruction, of the many roles of teachers, of professional and informal activities of the staff, of the whole school at work, of

schools at other levels and of other types and generally throughout the community. Assists ST in evaluating experiences and in gaining understanding and insight from them.

23. *Planned absence.* Gives ST increasingly longer periods of independent teaching as he seems ready, but does not just disappear. Plans carefully with ST for gradual increase in independent teaching, and arranges well beforehand with principal (and college supervisor when possible) for any half day or longer absence. Remains rather constantly with weak ST, one with very difficult group, or at the request of principal or college supervisor. When emergencies arise, leaves ST in his assigned situation and takes the substitute duty, unless ST is ready to profit from this specific opportunity and desires the experience.

24. *Full-day teaching.* When practicable, plans carefully with ST to teach his full schedule from one day up to a week or slightly over. Meanwhile observes ST only intermittently, but is available for consultation and supports ST by indicating his readiness to assume any authority which cannot be delegated.

25. *Final evaluation.* Adapts his activities to pattern agreed upon with college supervisor including three-way conference, if desired. Confers with college supervisor, supplies significant anecdotal information and brief evaluation report as may be requested. Arranges final informal conference helping ST to evaluate his total experience and lay plans for transition to regular teaching and for later professional growth. When requested by the college, decides on grade to recommend for ST, holds final formal conference, and writes recommendation for the placement office.

The Role of the College Supervisor

Confusion over the role of the college supervisor of student teaching is scarcely less than that over the work of the cooperating teacher. But in sharp contrast to the extensive literature for the cooperating teacher, writings about the function of the college supervisor have appeared only in the last ten years and the first book is now scheduled for publication. Again, teaching experience gives no assurance that a person is well qualified as a college supervisor, but training programs for this special function are very rare.

Few people really understand the legal and philosophical issues involved when a college employee steps out of his line of authority and begins operating in an entirely separate public school. The anomaly is that the college supervisor has authority over the student teacher and evaluates his work, but the public school teacher has authority over the teaching-learning situation and can and should decide what can be delegated to the student teacher. Nevertheless, many able and well-prepared college and public school teachers do make this joint arrangement work very satisfactorily.

A detailed analysis of the function of the college supervisor is included here in the hope that it will be helpful in clarifying his role. The statements are synthesized from all of the lists of functions known to this writer. Again, the pattern varies somewhat from one institution to another, but the basic ideas can be adapted easily to most organizations, for some college staff member must carry all of these functions. In addition to the use of ST for student teacher, the cooperating teacher is identified by CT.

Liaison agent between college and schools

1. Interprets the college program and college needs with particular reference to student teaching and related experiences.

2. Works actively to promote good working relationships among all the personnel involved in the experience phases of teacher education.

3. Assists professional personnel in understanding their roles in teacher education and especially defines the ST's role for the ST and for all others concerned.

4. Coordinates the program of student teaching and related experiences in given geographical areas within the limits of his assignment.

5. Serves as a "trouble-shooter" for the college to resolve serious problems relating to student teaching and to facilitate the improvement in general school-college relationships.

Placement and planning

1. Works as a public relations consultant visiting schools and teachers, constantly searching for quality schools and additional able CTs.

2. Proposes best possible placement for each ST and assists in completing the placement negotiations.

3. Develops an over-all plan for the professional experiences of given groups of STs and for the working relationships of the particular staff members involved.

4. Cooperates closely with principals in completing ST assignments, in planning for orientation of STs to the school and community, in setting up a good program of experiences for and guidance of STs, and in studying and resolving problem situations.

5. When necessary, and after careful study, recommends to college authorities a change in placement or the removal of a ST in a professional manner so as to protect the integrity of all concerned.

Relations with cooperating teachers

1. Gets acquainted with CT before ST arrives, if possible.

2. Provides CT with professional and personal information on ST, on the nature of the assignment and its relation to the college curriculum, and on the working relations which should be beneficial.

3. Confers as frequently as circumstances permit with CT to assist him since he is responsible for the actual day-to-day guidance of the ST's activities.

4. When desirable, confers with CT by telephone and through correspondence.

5. When appropriate, holds three-way conferences with CT and ST (sometimes four-way, including principal or other staff member) to facilitate the setting of goals, planning, evaluation, the arranging of additional experiences, and the resolving of problems.

6. Assists CT in planning a variety of activities and procedures to stimulate and increase professional growth of ST.

7. When appropriate, holds group conferences with two or more CTs to assist them in their work with STs, and to open channels for evaluating the program and sharing suggestions.

Supervision of student teachers

1. As circumstances and load assignments permit, serves in a counselor relationship with STs before, during, and after student teaching.

2. Acquaints himself with the professional and personal background of each ST.

3. Holds pre-student-teaching conferences with STs, preferably both on- and off-campus to help them prepare for their experiences and to orient them to particular schools and their philosophies. When necessary, assists in completing arrangements for housing, transportation, and the like.

4. Visits each school very early in the term, checking the adequacy of the placements and the expectations of the chief members of each student-teaching "team."

5. On the first and second visit tries to check on the adjustment and apparent adequacy of each ST.

6. Assists STs in resolving problems of adjustment and relationships throughout the experience.

7. Provides STs with a "safety valve" opportunity by being a good listener and confidante on problems and matters which STs prefer not to discuss in the school community.

8. Conducts or assists with a series of group seminars to lead STs in discussing their major problems and needs, to direct them in securing material, and in intellectualizing their experiences so as to develop maximum understanding and competency.

9. As circumstances dictate, holds individual or small group conferences with STs following observation of them. Includes CT when appropriate and constantly recognizes the broad scope of the CT's responsibility for direction and daily supervision.

10. When appropriate, regularly invites college content and methods instructors to accompany him when observing STs and conferring with them.

Evaluation of student teachers

1. Assists CT in planning and carrying through a program of evaluation of ST and developing ST's self-evaluation.

2. Collects data for evaluation through several observations of

ST and in conferences with CT, ST, and other members of the student-teaching team.

3. Evaluates ST's reports and materials and those provided by CT.

4. Makes final evaluation, determines grade, holds final conference with ST, submits grade to proper official, and writes recommendation for the teacher placement office.

Service to schools

1. Provides on-call supervisory service in all aspects of the teacher-education program.

2. Gives requested professional service to the schools, as circumstances permit, as a specialist in teaching methods and assists with suggestions or referrals on matters of information, materials, equipment, and so on.

3. Promotes and actively participates in a varied program of in-service education to assist public school personnel develop their competency in guiding the activities of STs.

Service at the college

1. Helps college staff understand and respect the schools' professional integrity, their needs, their proper role in teacher education, and helps college staff relate properly to school personnel.

2. Assists the college in developing and modifying professional programs in response to problems and changing conditions in the schools and communities and to the suggestions of school personnel.

3. Assists in the continuous evaluation of the student-teaching and experience program and in recommending changes.

4. Works for cooperation between professional and content departments by using content instructors and specialists as consultants in the student-teaching program.

5. Teaches courses and gives other service on campus when supervision of STs is less than a full assignment. When public school personnel are employed as part-time college supervisors the balance of their load may be in the school system.

The Role of the Principal

The third member of this student-teaching team is the principal of a school to which students are assigned. Only very recently has the importance of this role been recognized, and even less attention is given to it in the literature. Of all the persons in the school situation the principal is the one who can most effectively set the tone for a professional climate that is so important to the proper functioning of all these interrelationships. Of course, not all principals will find it possible to do all these things, but a principal can study the list and decide on those items which he can find time to do.

This analysis also is a synthesis based on current lists and would vary somewhat under different organizational patterns. The individual functions are presented more briefly than was the case for the two previous positions, but an attempt has been made to include every function currently noted in the literature. Again abbreviations have been used for cooperating teacher (CT) and student teacher (ST).

Relationships between college, school, and community

1. Interprets the teacher-education program to faculty, students, parents, and the general community, emphasizing the nature and importance of student teaching, and enlisting their support.

2. Maintains open channels of communication between college, school, and community. Takes time to meet and confer with college supervisors.

3. Assists college coordinator in introducing teacher-education activities into the school, and in the initial selection of CTs.

4. Assists college supervisor in becoming oriented to the school, its policies, the community, and to state programs and procedures applicable to teacher-education functions. Assists in locating and assigning conference space for college supervisor(s).

5. Participates actively in the placement process and gives final approval to all teacher-education students to be assigned in his school.

6. When appropriate, introduces STs to the school, the school clientele, and the community.

7. Assists in resolving differences in philosophy between school and college.

8. Works with school and college personnel to resolve problem cases and reach sound professional decisions in the best interests of the pupils.

9. Works with other school and college personnel to improve teacher-education programs.

10. Opens channels to make possible the occasional use of college supervisors as general consultants to the school.

Relationships with school faculty

1. Leads the faculty in a study of their role in teacher-education and especially with STs.

2. Counsels with teachers on their selection as CTs and encourages the best qualified to serve the profession in this way.

3. Gives STs professional status and integrates them as temporary staff members into the faculty family by inviting them to professional and social meetings of the staff and to community functions whenever conditions make it appropriate.

4. Counsels with teachers about their STs.

5. Counsels with teachers to assist them in providing their pupils with a well-balanced learning situation during STs' presence in the school.

6. Assists CTs and STs in arranging observations and special experiences in his school, other schools, and throughout the community.

7. Supports teachers and works closely with them on problems of weak STs and those arising because of the presence of the student-teaching program.

8. Encourages CTs to experiment and explore new approaches both in working with STs and with their classes during ST assignment.

9. When possible and appropriate readjusts teacher loads and provides released time for CTs to hold conferences, especially three-way and four-way conferences which include a college supervisor.

10. When appropriate, especially in large schools, delegates to

some staff member the responsibility for coordinating the teacher-education functions of the school.

11. Assists the faculty in building up the school professional library with materials designed to assist CTs and STs.

12. Assists his CTs in attending conferences with other CTs, meetings on teacher education in the area and at the college, and in attending informal and formal classes for improving their understanding and skill in working with prospective teachers.

Relationships with student teachers

1. Welcomes STs in initial conference to orient them to the school, its philosophy, policies, and its community.

2. Directs the preparation of specific materials for STs and suggests the use and adaptation of other items for them.

3. Gives general supervision of the STs, observing them sufficiently to be familiar with the quality of their work.

4. Orients STs to the work of the principal and the general operation of the school.

5. As opportunity presents itself, counsels with STs on professional matters, career choices, seeking a position, professional organizations, and the like.

6. Exercises constant care both to avoid exploitation of STs and to protect the best interests of the pupils.

Division of Responsibility

In as complex an operation as the program of student teaching, it is inevitable for some member of the team to misunderstand his role, to fail to carry his own role, or to take on the role of another. Probably the most common area of misunderstanding and uncertainty is in the division of responsibility between the cooperating teacher and the college supervisor. Teachers frequently ask, "Should the college supervisor do this, or do that?" Drawing on past experience an effort has been made to identify some of the common areas of uncertainty and to delineate the exact responsibilities for each position in these critical areas. The following chart is designed to assist those working in teacher-education to identify their roles more clearly and to direct their efforts more effectively, although institutional adaptations may be necessary at several points.

A Suggested Division Between the College Supervisor (CS)
and the Cooperating Teacher (CT)
of the Responsibility for Supervising a Student Teacher (ST)

College Supervisor's Responsibility	Joint Responsibility	Cooperating Teacher's Responsibility
Placement:		
Proposes the best possible placement for a given ST.	Principal confers with CS, CT, or both on placement.	Gives approval or disapproval of the request for the assignment of a ST as desirable or undesirable for that student at that time.
Information exchange:		
Provides CT with broad dimensions of ST's experience, professional and personal data, summary of college program, and proper channels to contact college.	ST gives such information as schedule, address and telephone number to both CS and CT.	Treats information on ST confidentially. Shares personal interests and preferences with ST.
Initial period:		
Checks the adequacy of placement with ST and CT, and helps the CT set up a desirable plan of activities for each ST.	Participates in two-way or three-way planning conferences.	Helps the ST feel accepted and wanted, and directs a carefully planned program of increasingly responsible induction activities.
Observation:		
Visits the school regularly and maintains frequent contact with the CT and ST.	Observes the ST at work.	In a team relationship CT remains with ST approximately 80 per cent of the time with planned absence to promote ST independence.
Conferences:		
Conducts initial and continuing group seminar on- or off-campus. Confers with ST following each observation.	Either or both CT and CS hold informal and arranged conferences with ST.	Continues daily informal conferences for planning and evaluation, plus frequent scheduled conferences. Calls on CS for suggestions and assistance.

THE RESPONSIBILITY FOR SUPERVISING A STUDENT TEACHER (*Cont.*)

College Supervisor's Responsibility	Joint Responsibility	Cooperating Teacher's Responsibility
ST Relationships:		
Helps ST resolve any problems of relationships with all persons involved. Helps ST understand differences in philosophy between school and college.	Helps ST solve some of his own professional and related personal problems.	Supports ST and maintains a permissive climate with ST as respected professional associate. Checks to be sure ST operates within official school policies.
Inadequate ST:		
Confers with principal and CT when serious problems arise. Arranges for the removal of ST when such a decision is made.	Keeps the channels of communication open both ways. Both CT and CS protect the best interest of the pupils.	Keeps the CS and principal informed of ST's deficiences. Teaches temporarily while case is studied, and ST observes CT and other teachers.
Evaluation:		
Develops estimate of ST's progress from reports of CT and observations. Gathers evidence from all parties concerned, decides on a final grade, and reports it to the Registrar. Holds final evaluation conference with ST. Writes a recommendation for the placement office.	Carries on a continuous program of evaluation of the ST's progress and the effectiveness of his planning jointly with him, including three-way conferences. Helps ST develop self-evaluation.	Gathers data for the CS to be used in the final evaluation of the ST. Holds informal mid-term stock-taking conference, and informal final conference directed toward adjustment in a regular teaching position.

Summary

The history of student teaching clearly illustrates that patterns of organization and levels of responsibility have changed and seem to be constantly evolving. In the team relationship for the supervision of student teaching, the public school teacher serving as a cooperating teacher is the key figure, and must carry the full responsibility and authority for directing the day-to-day activities of the student teacher as illustrated by the chart on page 49. Whenever at some future time the public schools can be supported adequately by the state or the federal government to provide excellent laboratories for teacher education, the colleges should be able to structure a theoretically defensible and efficiently operating team for supervision. But even without outside support, a careful analysis of the roles of each of the members of the student-teaching team could do much to improve the quality of student teaching. A sound program can be provided by educators if they have a clear understanding of function, skill in human relations, and a high sense of the importance of building a genuine profession of teaching.

CHAPTER V

High Quality Student Teaching

The expression "high quality student teaching" is often found in the literature, but defining it adequately and getting agreement on the definition is most difficult. In the last decade the Association for Student Teaching sponsored the development of two definitive descriptions of quality programs in student teaching but neither have received wide acceptance. The profession as a whole has not yet developed a satisfactory answer to the question, "What should be the nature of a high quality student-teaching experience?"

Generally the approach to quality has been pursued on a local basis and has tended to be fragmentary and intermittent. The special contribution of the Flowers Report was that it gave the profession a "grand design" and dramatized the need for a comprehensive quality program. Unfortunately, many college staff members seem to have concerned themselves more with the specific conditions and mechanical procedures proposed in the report than with the nature of the student-teaching experience itself. Many teachers would be shocked if they realized that a student-teaching program which provides excellent conditions for learning can be used most effectively to prepare teachers for any "ism," any type of society, and even for the worst social purposes.

The real quality question is, "What is the essence of good teaching, its philosophy, its purpose, its character?" Good programs of student teaching provide a good setting for learning, but the character of that learning is determined by the ideals, aspirations, understandings, behavior, and instruction given by the people who work with the student teacher. Since the desired learning is to produce effective teachers, the task of determining the quality of the product is also difficult. Junge points to this in the last principle of a list in the 1962 Yearbook of the Association for Student Teaching, thus:

> Guideline XIII. Competence in teaching is a far more complex, far more demanding level of performance than we have been accustomed to recognize.[1]

Until more adequate criteria of effective teaching are available, the minimum essential is for a well-developed theoretical rationale for excellent teaching. Obviously the development of such concepts is beyond the scope of this book, but it must be recognized that a program of student teaching designed to follow generally accepted guiding principles will not in and of itself produce superior teachers. The student-teaching program must be integrated into a well-designed total curriculum, and then good student teaching can make a major contribution to good teacher education.

Currently there are several major research projects which are using various approaches into the nature of teaching itself, while studies of learning and learning theory are discovering and exploring very provocative ideas. In 1963 the Association for Student Teaching departed from its usual pattern of topics and published a yearbook in the area of quality of teaching and learning, entitled, *Concern for the Individual in Student Teaching.* Chapter VI reports on the nature of teaching and Chapter VIII discusses value development; and from such analyses the reader can get an introduction into these very significant areas. Another organization, the Association for Supervision and Curriculum Development (ASCD) has taken real leadership in exploring concepts and implications from such related disciplines as psychology, sociology, and anthropology, reporting the results through yearbooks and bulletins. Unfortunately, there is considerable reason to doubt whether the typical classroom teacher has yet been influenced by these efforts. If the usual cultural lag can be shortened, the prospects are excellent that these new areas of knowledge can have a salutory impact both on the procedures in student teaching and on understanding and practice in the entire range of teaching.

---

[1] Charlotte W. Junge, "A Rationale for Professional Laboratory Experiences," *The Outlook in Student Teaching,* Forty-First Yearbook (Cedar Falls, Iowa: The Association for Student Teaching, 1962), p. 155.

Principles and Standards

In the years following World War I, some of the recorded attempts at improvement in student teaching were analyses of what teachers did and projections of the tasks which student teachers should try to include during their assignment. The earliest standards of the AATC were very sketchy and included only hours, credits, and the proportion of time to be spent on class instruction. Today both of these mechanistic approaches seem quite inadequate except for a restricted operational analysis. But during the 1930's, which was a period rich in the development of new ideas, several impressive sets of proposed principles appeared.

In 1939 Patterson presented eight principles in an effort to redefine the values and functions of student teaching. Although this is probably one of the best such lists yet developed, still, conservatives of today both in education and in social theory probably would find some items unacceptable. These principles, when considered with the concepts now emerging from the related disciplines, are a most provocative stimulus to those responsible for curriculum development both in student teaching and the total teacher-education program. Three examples will serve to illustrate this point:

> Experiences in student teaching should be so selected and utilized as to develop a deep concern for the social, economic, and spiritual tensions of the surrounding culture as they affect the development of children and establish some competence in using these cultural conflicts for instructional purposes.[2]

This principle seems especially appropriate to the efforts now being initiated to prepare teachers for children in the culturally deprived areas of our large cities, such as those currently in progress at several divisions of The City University of New York.

> The dominating spirit in the student-teaching program should be consistent with the spirit of experimentation, broadly interpreted, and developed in a manner consistent with the conception of supervision as "counselled self-direction."[3]

---

2 Allen D. Patterson, "Redefining the Values and Functions of Student Teaching," *Supervisors of Student Teaching*, Nineteenth Annual Session (Cleveland, February 27, 28, 1939), p. 38.

3 *Ibid.*, p. 40.

The above principle suggests that cooperating teachers re-examine their own standard of permissiveness in their relations with student teachers, and also that the college supervisors and instructors of methods courses be less rigid in their insistence that student teachers always follow exactly the procedures taught at the college.

> Student teaching, although directed by a cooperatively developed philosophy of education, should acquaint the student with the conflicting points of view and practice in educational philosophy, psychology, sociology, etc., and enable student teachers to resolve these conflicts in a personally satisfying way so that they can function effectively as teachers in transitional public schools.[4]

In his discussion of this principle, Patterson strongly urged that students have actual experience in schools conducted under differing philosophies and practices. The difficulty of accomplishing this has increased over the years, and this is another objective which might be facilitated by a library of teletape or sound film reproductions of many different classroom episodes.

Another significant list of suggested guiding principles for the organization and operation of a student-teaching program is that by Schorling in the 1935 yearbook of the National Society of College Teachers of Education.[5] The entire yearbook is most unusual in that it is a critical review of the report of the National Survey of the Education of Teachers. Supported by a federal appropriation, the survey was essentially a statistical analysis of all activities in teacher education with recommendations for change made by some of the key members of the staff. Believed by this writer to have been the only comprehensive national study of teacher education, its impact was very disappointing. Whether this was due to the limited resources of colleges in the depression decade or to inadequacies in the study and the report itself is difficult to judge.

On the other hand, the Schorling list of 14 principles and its accompanying discussion anticipate many of the suggestions to be found in most studies and proposals up to the present. Although

4 *Ibid.*, p. 40.
5 Raleigh Schorling, "Directed Teaching," *The Education of Teachers,* Yearbook Number XXIII, National Society of College Teachers of Education (Chicago: The University of Chicago Press, 1935), pp. 127–185.

developed by the yearbook committee and the writer, the proposals had been critically reviewed and supported by a panel of widely recognized administrators of student-teaching programs. The proposed program recommends a comprehensive range of experiences, including contact with most of the instructional and noninstructional duties of the teacher, selective admission of only students superior to the general college population, provision for adjustment to individual needs especially during the induction phase, a systematic program of evaluation, adequate protection for the pupils, and the addition of a probationary internship. Special emphasis was given to the selection and preparation of the critic teachers (as they were called at that time) and to the importance of their being skilled in their special functions with student teachers and particularly in the use of conference techniques.

One of Schorling's guiding principles is notable now as then, and its importance for the future can scarcely be overemphasized:

> Principle 12. The program of directed teaching should develop in the student teacher the spirit of experimentation so that as a teacher he will be able to modify subject matter and methods to fit ever-changing needs.[6]

Only one of the principles has really been made obsolete by the events of the ensuing years, but even it raises an issue that is still an issue—that of who controls the school and thus the nature of instruction (see Chapter IV).

> Principle 11. An institution should not give credit for directed teaching unless that institution exercises adequate control over the directed teaching situation.[7]

The almost complete shift to the use of cooperating public schools rather than laboratory schools makes the official relationship different from that suggested in the above principle, but the objectives suggested in the discussion which followed are still most appropriate:

> The right kind of organization will (1) provide an adequate number of cooperating schools, and (2) make the arrangement mutually profitable for both parties entering into the agreement.[8]

---

[6] *Ibid.*, p. 169.
[7] *Ibid.*, p. 168.
[8] *Ibid.*, p. 169.

Schorling could scarcely have anticipated the great expansion in the use of public schools as student-teaching laboratories, but more serious concern for this last point plus the application of good theoretical principles of teacher education and administration could develop far more efficient and beneficial laboratories than those currently common throughout the country.

In an even more prophetic vein Schorling comments on the difficulty of helping critic teachers to make it a habit to read research literature and "face the important task of blowing away the chaff and revealing the grain of truth,"[9] and he also recognizes a fundamental problem of research which is only now beginning to be remedied:

> The chief obstacle to improvement of the curriculum and of instructional procedures is the fragmentary character of research studies dealing with learning and the neglect of basic, integrated studies of the school subjects.[10]

This most stimulating chapter concludes with a detailed analysis of a true professional internship with a set of guiding principles which should be most helpful to those designing fifth-year programs.

As has previously been noted, the Flowers Report unquestionably includes the most significant set of guiding principles and recommendations for program development yet to appear. In the concluding chapter four proposals are given as a base on which to build a sound program of professional laboratory experiences:

> . . . a program of professional education where growth in ability to act-on-thinking and to guide others in developing this ability are central.

> . . . professional laboratory experiences are a resource turned to by students and instructors to give meaning to ideas and to help the learner more clearly see the implementation of those ideas.

> . . . professional laboratory experiences which students have a share in selecting, for which they see some need in their plan of work, and from which emerge new needs and new purposes that give direction to next steps in the college program.

> . . . professional laboratory experiences which provide opportuni-

---

[9] *Ibid.*, p. 145.
[10] *Ibid.*, p. 145.

ties for the student to evaluate his ability to function effectively in the range of activities of the teacher of today.[11]

If college faculties could have more studious concern for establishing programs which really meet these conditions rather than the more mechanical guiding principles, the results might be most salutory.

As a guide to colleges in improving their programs, the report then proceeds to delineate some of the program details which would make possible a climate and conditions in which students could have high quality experiences. The scope of these program details can be judged by the six major criteria listed here, but which in the report are developed much more fully:

(1) Direct laboratory experiences, therefore, should be an integral part of the work of each of the four years of college.

(2) The professional programs should be so designed as to afford opportunity for responsible participation in all of the major activities of today's teacher.

(3) Both assignment to and length of time spent in a given situation or type of laboratory experience will vary with individuals. Each contact should be long enough to help the student achieve the purposes for which he entered upon the experience.

(4) Guidance of professional laboratory experiences should at all times be in terms of basic educational principles rather than patterns.

(5) . . . guidance of these experiences must be the joint responsibility of the laboratory teacher and the college representative most closely associated with the student's activities in the laboratory situation.

(6) There is need for laboratory facilities sufficiently extensive to provide for each student contact with normal situations; varied enough to provide contacts with different pupil groups, curriculum and administrative organizations; and located for student convenience and staff accessibility.[12]

The first recommendation is now controversial with the development of teacher-education programs of four years of liberal arts plus one of professional studies, or two years of general education and three years emphasizing the professional and teaching-subject

---

[11] Sub-Committee of the Standards and Surveys Committee, *School and Community Laboratory Experiences in Teacher Education* (Oneonta, N.Y.: American Association of Teachers Colleges, 1948), pp. 317–320.

[12] *Ibid.*, pp. 322–330. (Italics removed and numbers added for clarity.)

courses. The second and fourth proposals are generally accepted but their implementation is far from universal. The third is often accepted as an ideal but is almost totally neglected in the lock-step progression of students through precise course and time requirements. The fifth is the controversial issue of responsibility for supervision developed in the previous chapter. In many colleges pyramiding enrollments and accidents of geography are so restrictive that the really significant aspect of the sixth proposal—comprehensiveness of student experience—often is largely ignored.

Since the publication of the Flowers Report, many other statements of principles, proposals, and standards have been prepared, but none have the depth of analysis or have had the impact upon the profession of that report. In general the later statements have tended to be restricted to certain areas or institutions or to be rather quantitative and concerned primarily with operational details.

Although there is still a real need for a comprehensive theoretical base for professional laboratory experiences (see Chapter II), actually the limitations on quality are not due primarily to a lack of clear objectives. Rather, they seem due primarily to the inability of the profession to take the guides that are available, and to find sufficient human and material resources with which to develop a high quality program.

Hindrances to Quality

In an area as complex and diverse as this, the hindrances and problems are many. Brief consideration will be given to several of the more troublesome areas in addition to the three major concerns which have already been considered in some detail: lack of a theoretical base for these experiences, lack of a clear differentiation of the roles of supervisory personnel, and the difficulties in designing adequate experiences and programs.

Problems

Terminology. From its beginning this field has suffered because of a confused and inadequate set of names for its personnel and their relationships. Accurate communication is very difficult. Several of the well-accepted terms have unfortunate connotations, and the efficiency of many people suffers from a misunderstanding of their roles and duties. More than just a selection of acceptable terms is needed, and especially just now when so many experiences are being developed and combined in new ways. A major national organization of prestige could render real service to the profession by a study which could identify needs, resolve conflicts, simplify terms and propose some more appropriate labels.

Confusion over a new term in teacher education has been accentuated by Conant's use of "clinical professor" to designate a professor of the teaching of a secondary subject (methods instructor) who also supervises student teachers in that field. Both this author in the 1959 Yearbook of the Association for Student Teaching[13] and Robert B. Bush in the Fort Collins Conference Report[14] use "clinical professor" to describe a superior classroom teacher who is also very skillful in working with student teachers. The clinical professor in the health professions is usually an active practitioner who also supervises the work of neophytes in that profession. In teacher education Conant takes him out of the classroom, but suggests that he return to a public school to teach every three or four years.[15] Such an experience for a methods instructor is a sound idea, and it has been done on rare occasions, but this proposal is scarcely practical on any routine or universal basis. Perhaps, the best possible use of the term "clinical professor" would be to dignify the well-trained, experienced cooperating teacher in a public school who achieves real distinction in his role in teacher education.

Adequate teacher-education laboratories.   Far too large a group of colleges face the dilemma that neither the college nor the available public schools have the resources to provide good quality teacher-education laboratories. The profession and the public must accept the fact that in such cases either the support must be provided to make laboratory situations adequate or the college ought to eliminate its teacher-education curriculum. A great many colleges

---

13 L. O. Andrews, "The Task Ahead," *The Supervising Teacher,* Thirty-Eighth Yearbook (Cedar Falls, Iowa: The Association for Student Teaching, 1959), p. 115.

14 Robert B. Bush, "Self-Determination and Self-Regulation in the Profession of Teaching," *Professional Imperatives: Expertness and Self-Determination,* Official Report of the Fort Collins Conference (Washington, D.C.: National Commission on Teacher Education and Professional Standards, 1962), pp. 45–46.

15 James B. Conant, *The Education of American Teachers* (New York: McGraw-Hill Book Company, 1963), pp. 140, 142–44.

desperately need additional support to improve the program of some or all of the schools that receive their students.

Selection, preparation, recognition, and compensation for co-operating teachers. Despite numerous studies, doctoral dissertations, and great effort to develop sound procedures, much of the practice of selecting cooperating teachers is still haphazard at best, with some approaches simply professionally disgraceful. The reasons are numerous, but perhaps the two most common are lack of understanding of sound criteria and failure to give this function the time and attention needed.

The lack of preparation for the highly specialized service of cooperating teachers has already been mentioned. In recognition of this problem the Association for Student Teaching has established a study group, the Commission on Professional Education for the Supervising Teacher. A great variety of procedures are used in working at this staggering task, including courses, conferences, seminars, textbooks, monographs, special handbooks, bulletins, and individual assistance. Again the lack of uniformity is disturbing; the teachers in some states, in some areas and some schools are well provided for, while others receive little or no assistance. The number of colleges offering special courses in the supervision of student teaching is growing, but is still ridiculously small.

The quality of student teaching will be little better than the competence of the classroom teacher who directs this experience. As suggested earlier the clinical professor in the health professions plays an important and highly respected role. Such a professor needs to be a skillful practitioner, to be able to demonstrate and teach sound practice, and to be competent in directing and evaluating the work of beginners. The profession of teaching should expect no less of its clinical professor teachers, but the problem becomes much more acute in education because of the rapid turnover in the profession and the hundreds of thousands of new teachers who must complete preparation and be certified each year.

Nowhere in this whole field is diversity greater than in the recognition of the service of cooperating teachers and in the fringe benefits which colleges are able to give in lieu of more substantial compensation or status. If these attempts at recognition were in addition to adequate pay, one could support such gestures as desirable and proper. But the profession cannot hope to stimulate adequate personal and professional development through token benefits such as giving college rank as critic teachers; listing names in catalogs; library, social, athletic and cultural privileges; gifts of teaching materials and professional books; in-service conferences and courses; free tuition; occasional free meals; or payments ranging upwards from $5 to $300 per student teacher with the mode around $50.

Competent college supervisors and administrators of student teaching. As college enrollments increase, the competition for additional staff grows ever more keen. Most new college staff members assigned to supervise student teaching will be recruited directly from the public schools or drafted from other teaching assignments, because only a mere handful of universities have formal programs for the preparation of administrators and supervisors of student teaching.

Teachers' organizations and other professional groups are demanding, and rightly so, that college supervisors have experience as certificated public school teachers and that they be familiar with instruction at the levels and in the subjects in which they expect to direct student teachers. But here again, experience of one kind does not, ipso facto, make them competent to guide and direct the student teacher in this important period of his professional growth. Probably the only practical approach to this problem for the present is some type of team grouping of supervisors with experienced team leaders responsible for in-service development. Graduate training programs in this area should also be expanded and increased in number.

The position of director or coordinator of student teaching (or of field laboratory experiences) is subject to the same problems of recruitment as that of the college supervisor. A more fundamental difficulty exists, however, in that these administrative posts suffer from a lack of status, and the incumbents all too often use them as convenient way stations on the road to more prestigeful senior professorships and administrative posts. The result is a real shortage of career people for the long-range leadership so badly needed. Deciding which is cause and which is result is indeed difficult, but lack of adequate preparation probably produces both low status and a feeling of insecurity and dislike for the work.

The fact that the administrator in the student-teaching area is faced with perennial budget shortages and must put up with unsatisfied demands from faculty, school people, and students, about which he is almost powerless to do anything, probably affects his attitude adversely. Furthermore, operating a program in this field requires the administrator to meet deadlines constantly, and by any standard the work load is most burdensome. A high quality program is not likely to emerge without some margin of time for skilled administrative leadership to give to research, to program development, and to public relations.

Evaluation of performance. Nearly all persons involved with student teaching tend either to dislike or to feel inadequate (or both) in the area of the evaluation of student-teacher performance. Infrequently an experienced and skillful cooperating teacher provides a student teacher with an excellent experience both through direct evaluation and growth in self-evaluation. Too often others neglect doing any real evaluation with the student teacher because of their own distaste for it. Here is another major area which may be affected considerably by developing research, and which, in any event, deserves a great deal more study and attention than it has received.

Legal. Questions as to the legal status of the student teacher have been raised most infrequently, even in states which have comprehensive bulletins describing desirable programs and standards for personnel and for approval of institutions. Most surprising, actually, is the small number of cases involving student teachers which are reported as having gone through the courts. Professional workers in many fields are disturbed by the growing number of malpractice suits and all kinds of damage suits against them, and the size of the judgments is sometimes fantastic. As a consequence, professional liability insurance for teachers has become commonplace in the last few years.

Temporarily, some social forces may be holding back the flood of legal actions against student teachers—factors such as the public awareness of the teacher shortage and general agreement that a prospective teacher should have some guided probationary experience. Unfortunately there is good reason to believe that this freedom from legal action may not last indefinitely. Specialists in school law recommend that each state seek legislation setting forth clearly the legal status of the student teacher, or arrange to issue some type of certificate to each student teacher. This type of proposal might well be combined in a more comprehensive bill covering all phases of a state program for student teaching.

Laws, certificates, standards, competent personnel, and good schools cannot in and of themselves produce quality student teaching, but certainly they can provide conditions under which the teacher-education team can work more effectively to provide high quality experiences for student teachers.

Issues. In addition to hindrances and problems, there are many national, state, and local issues in relation to student teaching that may force those in positions of responsibility to make choices directly or by default. Several of them are considered or referred to in other parts of this book, but these and others are summarized here to make possible a better overview. This group of critical questions appears to this writer to have a genuine bearing on developing quality programs, and some issues are likely to come to a sharp focus here and there throughout the country.

1. *Responsibility for providing good laboratories in teacher education.* Should the primary responsibility for developing and providing adequate teacher-education laboratories for all colleges be assumed by the state; or by the colleges and the public schools jointly; or by the public schools alone?

2. *Financial responsibility for teacher-education laboratories.* Should the additional cost of providing adequate teacher-education laboratories for all colleges be assumed by the state; or by the state with matching federal funds; or by the colleges and public schools jointly; or by the public schools alone?

3. *Responsibility for coordinating and regulating the operation and administration of teacher-education laboratories.* Should the administration and operation of teacher-education laboratories in the public schools be coordinated and regulated primarily through state controls; or by the cooperative effort of local agencies with some leadership and assistance from both official and professional agencies at the state level?

4. *Responsibility for the development and operation of teacher-education laboratory experiences.* Should the laboratory phases of teacher education remain a part of the college-controlled curriculum; or should the total laboratory phase of teacher education be operated by the state as a part of probationary experiences in professional service; or turned over completely and directly to the public schools as a part of in-service education?

5. *Responsibility for the supervision of student teaching.* Should the responsibility for the supervision of student teaching be organized by the colleges as a joint responsibility with the public schools; or should the responsibility be delegated to the public schools completely?

6. *Standards for supervisory personnel.* Should the profession seek to regulate and upgrade the various types of supervisory personnel through state regulations and certification; or through some state-wide suggested guidelines and recommended programs; or through some voluntary standards developed and operated by a professional organization?

7. *Responsibility for college supervision.* Should the colleges assign their supervisory staff to work as general or special area supervisors? That is, should faculty members be prepared and assigned as general college supervisors over student teachers in any subject area or grade level; or should they be assigned to supervise student teachers in a single subject field or narrow range of fields; or, should general supervisors be assigned to cover just a few related subject fields and have several specialists in these same specific fields serving as consultants?

8. *Number and types of advanced laboratory experiences.* Should prospective teachers have an integrated program (extending to five or more years) which would include student teaching and a professional internship; or should they have only either (a) undergraduate student teaching or (b) post-graduate internship-apprenticeship; or should they have post-graduate student teaching and an internship?

9. *Relation of types of experience to future employment.* Should prospective teachers go through a professional curriculum and experiences designed to prepare them for service in schools with the best program, the best teaching, and the best equipment; or should they be prepared for a wide range of types and quality of schools;

or for certain types of schools as a sort of early preservice specialization?

Research inadequacies. The amount of research done in the area of student teaching 20 to 40 years ago is most surprising as is the apparently small impact these results have had on improvement in quality. Many of the early studies were surveys of practice or attempts to measure relationships and make comparisons but with most inadequate techniques, as can be judged by reviewing Mead's encyclopedic volume, *Supervised Student-Teaching.*[16]

John U. Michaelis in his review of research on student teaching in the Third edition of the *Encyclopedia of Educational Research* summarizes the recent situation this way:

> The general status of critical, evaluative research on student teaching is poor. This is due to a lack of interest in this area until recently and also to the difficulties in doing conclusive research in such a diverse and uncontrollable field of activity. . . . Available published literature is made up largely of articles based on opinion, descriptions of practice, recommendations of committees and commissions, surveys and related recommendations, and a few critical studies.[17]

College administrators of student teaching, faculty committees, and individuals often seek ideas to assist in the solution of practical problems in the operation of their programs. Therefore, these surveys of practice may have served as guides to changes in operational matters, but have had little influence otherwise. A graduate student recently wrote, "Many of the research studies concerning student teaching seemed to tell us little that we didn't already know," and this reaction may be another clue to the lack of influence of this research on practice.

A very considerable number of the doctor's dissertations in the area of student teaching have sought answers to practical problems, too, especially in the areas of the selection and improvement of school laboratories and the selection, special preparation, compen-

---

16 Arthur R. Mead, *Supervised Student-Teaching* (Richmond: Johnson Publishing Company, 1930).

17 John U. Michaelis, "Teacher Education–Student Teaching and Internship," *Encyclopedia of Educational Research* (New York: The Macmillan Company, 1960), pp. 1473–74.

sation, and work of the cooperating teachers and others in the supervisory team.

One easily gets the impression that few doctor's dissertations are reported extensively enough in the literature to have any impact on practice. As a check on this observation, the lists of dissertations for two years were scanned to identify those in the field of student teaching which from their titles might have conclusions and suggestions of more than local interest. The result was a list of eight submitted in 1958–59 and 13 in 1959–60, and these 21 authors were surveyed to see how many of them published magazine articles listed in the *Education Index* from July, 1959 through June, 1962. Not one of these new recipients of the doctor's degree had published an indexed monograph or magazine article on his research in the years immediately following the completion of the degree.

In recent years research in teacher education has received greatly increased support, especially from private foundations and the federal government. Experts in research techniques assure teacher educators that many of the stubborn problems of measurement and many variables can now be surmounted, and the exciting progress being made in research on the nature of teaching is stimulating the expansion of research more closely related to teacher education and student teaching. The results thus far are of rather limited significance but the outlook is very promising, and will be considered further in the next chapter.

Summary

Many college faculties have worked vigorously to improve the quality of their programs of student teaching and against the obstacles of rising numbers, distances, rapid staff turnover, and limited budgets. Definite gains have been made at some institutions, but there is no way to acquire a comprehensive picture either of quality or of change. The most concrete and observable gains are those which improve the conditions for student teaching such as extended assignments and improved preparation of cooperating teachers.

Most of the effort for improvement has been local and institutional, but there are a few observable general trends. Many more states now have statements suggesting good practices and procedures, some of which are used in evaluating institutions. In both states and local areas, groups are working to improve school-college relations, and often cities are allocating more central office staff time to coordinating teacher education. A small committee surveyed the accredited high schools in the 19 state area in which the North Central Association of Schools and Colleges operates and found that 70 of the 1029 high schools reduced the extracurricular load of teachers having student teachers, and 25 even assigned these teachers fewer classes.

Despite the constant barrage of criticism of teacher education, there is a growing awareness and understanding of the importance of teacher education on the part of both the profession and the public. The net effect of the many new programs, especially the internships and those which provide for alternating periods of service in the schools and study on campuses, has surely created more interest in change and more concern for the laboratory phases of teacher education.

But probably the most significant development, although certainly not the most spectacular, has been the increased awareness of many teachers of the importance of good interpersonal relations throughout the whole student-teaching program. After many years the writer now senses in his graduate classes for cooperating teachers a distinct improvement in their interest and sophistication in this area. Growing numbers of teachers have had training in guidance and counselling, and they can be helped to see the relationship of their new knowledge to their work with student teachers.

The impact is still limited, but the possibilities are encouraging. If teachers generally can secure a better background in the related disciplines and in interpersonal relations, they may become far more understanding of the learning process through which a student teacher moves and more skillful in the direction of his experiences.

CHAPTER VI

New Horizons in Student Teaching

The previous chapters have presented a review of the development of student teaching and some analysis of the current scene. Over a long period the record is one of great expansion and improvement in program, but there are still many problems and many issues needing attention today. With nearly 1200 colleges preparing teachers, and nearly all contending with rising enrollments, improvements in student teaching are not likely to be very rapid. There are many developments, efforts, and resources, which, if capitalized upon, can contribute much to the improvement of student teaching in the next decade or two, provided, of course, that there are not too many or too violent shifts of an international, military, economic, vocational, or social nature. Even a brief review of the history of student teaching reveals clearly that teacher education is such a vast operation that any major shift in the country will have a very observable effect on student teaching.

This chapter considers some of the present developments which may greatly affect student teaching in the years ahead.

The Tidal Wave of College Students

College enrollments are being influenced primarily by two factors —the gross number of births and the steadily advancing percentage of high school graduates who attend college. The depression years of the 1930's were characterized by continued low birth rates with 1933 having the lowest (this number was nearly doubled in most states in the year 1947). The trend since 1947 has been an uneven but generally gradual increase, and the annual number is leveling off at something like two and one-third times the number in 1933.

From these basic population facts stem several very important

91

inferences affecting teacher education. In the next few years new college faculty must be recruited largely from a numerically small population group born between 1933 and 1947, which explains in part the slow increase in the annual number of doctor's degrees being earned. College enrollments will continue to advance sharply since the number of youth aged 18 through 21 will almost double between 1960 and 1970. Advancing steadily through the grades, the largest wave of pupils has been the 1947 births and these students will move out of the high schools and into the colleges by 1965. While this wave was on its way through the public schools, large numbers of additional teachers were needed each year to teach the added number of pupils, but after 1964 increases will be more moderate and the demand will be chiefly for teacher replacements.

At some time in the next decade all signs point to an oversupply of newly certificated teachers for the secondary schools in most subject fields, but there will be a shortage of elementary school teachers for many years because more youth choose the secondary field and because large numbers of women elementary teachers leave the profession after brief service. Unless present trends shift markedly, the number of student teachers may more than double between 1960 and 1970. The proportion of experienced teachers who can be prepared to serve as cooperating teachers should rise slowly, but would probably increase more rapidly if salaries of all teachers should rise faster than the economy, and if a generous honorarium were paid to experienced cooperating teachers.

In the light of the population picture, colleges should consider several policy changes such as raising standards for admission to teacher education and for eligibility for student teaching; moving to a five-year integrated program for secondary teachers and later for elementary teachers; developing trial programs for student teaching *plus* internship for selected secondary education students prior to adopting new curricula; and exploring the use of a preliminary student-teaching experience as an additional method of screening entrants to the profession. Such developments as the above will further increase the demand for competent school and college personnel and for more public schools to provide high quality experiences for prospective teachers.

The Profession Proposes New Dimensions

In the post-war period, the profession of teaching has shown signs of increasing maturity by the organization of a number of important agencies to promote professional development and the improvement of teacher education. In 1946 the National Commission on Teacher Education and Professional Standards (TEPS) was established by the National Education Association. The Commission has had an increasing influence nationally, and through state and local commissions and committees this effort has begun to reach throughout the profession.

In 1959 TEPS established a task force which prepared a comprehensive blueprint for the future development of the profession, *New Horizons for the Teaching Profession,* which appeared in 1961. Admittedly controversial, the report presents proposals in five major areas: preparation, accreditation, certification, selection of entrants into the profession, and the responsibility of the profession for the enforcement of its standards. Certainly the report has intensified efforts for the improvement of the profession, although, of course, the resulting developments may take a form differing considerably from the proposal itself.

In the section on the preparation of professional personnel the report makes specific recommendations for student teaching and internship. The excerpts quoted here are some of the key statements and are further elaborated upon in the report itself:

> *A full-time period of student teaching is required in addition to the direct experiences which are a part of collegiate life and of in-course work.*
>> Provision should be made for at least one and possibly two periods of full-time student teaching.
>> The nature of the experiences to be included in student teaching should provide direct contact with the range of the educator's activities.
>> Observation as an experience separate from participation should come late rather than early in the student's program.
>> Student teaching should be under expert supervision, jointly carried by a representative of the college and the field situation.
> *An internship should be provided; it is, however, not a substitute for student teaching.*

Until more substantial evidence is available, there is need to experiment with varied patterns of internship.[1]

Organized in 1954, the National Council for Accreditation in Teacher Education (NCATE) is the only national agency responsible for evaluating and accrediting colleges which prepare teachers. The NCATE standards and guides are divided into seven areas of which Standard VI is "Professional Laboratory Experiences for School Personnel." This standard has evolved from a similar standard based upon the Flowers Report and used previously by the American Association of Colleges for Teacher Education (AACTE). In its present form it illustrates the difficulty of writing a standard in such a way that it really measures the quality of a program. The two paragraphs of Standard VI pertaining directly to student teaching are as follows:

> The professional laboratory experiences should culminate in a continuous period of student teaching so organized as to provide for a wide range of professional activities in which teachers should engage, and so administered as to assure that the activities contribute substantially to the learning of students. Facilities adequate to provide such experiences at a high level of effectiveness for the number of students involved should be provided. The working arrangement between the institution and the school(s) where student teaching is done should constitute a partnership which places appropriate responsibilities on school administrators, supervising teachers, and college supervisors for the supervision of student teachers.
>
> Adequate provisions for supervision by the college faculty should be made for all aspects of professional laboratory experiences including those prior to student teaching as well as student teaching itself.[2]

In their present form the *Standards and Guide* tend to elicit from the institutions primarily a description of program and a collection of statistical data. Many persons are disappointed in the failure of the standard to set forth a better description of desired practice and to obtain more data indicative of the quality of the program. The total NCATE standards are under study by different groups and it

---

[1] Margaret Lindsey, ed., *New Horizons for the Teaching Profession* (Washington, D.C.: National Commission on Teacher Education and Professional Standards, National Education Association, 1961), pp. 69–71.

[2] *Standards and Guide for Accreditation of Teacher Education* (Washington, D.C.: National Council for Accreditation of Teacher Education, 1960).

is hoped that Standard VI can be revised to work more effectively for program improvement in student teaching.

The work of NCATE, TEPS, and other organizations concerned with teacher education has definitely tended to open up lines of communication, with the result that teachers and administrators, especially many of those actively engaged in carrying forward the work of local, state, and national professional organizations, are far better informed about teacher education than they were even a few years ago. It may very well prove that the greatest resource available to assist with change and improvement in student teaching is the growing group of informed, concerned, and dedicated members of the profession.

A Suggested State Program

As with other aspects of student teaching the several states have the most diverse regulations and published programs, ranging from no statewide provisions whatsoever to comprehensive programs, including special training and state compensation for cooperating teachers. In recent years several states have completed plans or have groups actively at work developing such proposals.

Since interest is now so high in providing some leadership and direction from the state level, an informal synthesis has been made of topics and concerns which are included in present and proposed programs. State plans must of necessity be adapted to local problems and needs, and should certainly be developed cooperatively by groups with representation from the state department, colleges, public schools, teachers associations, and the public. The outline here could serve a planning committee as a checklist of types of topics, provisions, and actions which they might consider.

A Suggested Checklist of Provisions for a State Program on
Student Teaching and Professional Laboratory Experiences

1. Definitions of a system of acceptable terminology.
2. A detailed description of a comprehensive program of professional laboratory experiences and student teaching for teacher education. Provision should be made for acceptable variations and encouragement given for professionally directed exploration of new approaches.
3. A listing of all types of personnel involved in the laboratory phases

of teacher education, together with suggested guides for their selection, qualifications, status, and function.

4. Guiding principles for the operation of programs of professional laboratory experiences with special attention to the joint responsibility of schools and colleges. Emphasis should be on providing adequate laboratories for high quality experiences, while at the same time protecting the integrity and proper status of each of the institutions and types of personnel involved.

5. Included in state regulations governing teacher preparation institutions, provision for an approved program approach to plans of the colleges for direct experiences for prospective teachers. Each college would be required to develop its own plan of direct experiences adapted to its own teacher-education curriculum and the laboratory facilities available to it. Initially such plans could be submitted by the colleges, after approval by the respective school systems, and filed for information, study, and review by a joint professional group representing the state department, colleges, and public schools. After a period of trial and modification such plans would be officially approved by the proper state agency; and thereafter major modifications would be made in the same manner as changes in other aspects of teacher-education programs.

6. Legislative action to establish state responsibility for providing high quality professional laboratory experiences in the public schools. This action should provide state authority for the general direction and necessary controls sufficient to insure a good minimum program, and should delegate authority, duties, and leadership responsibilities to the proper agencies and officers. Further, it should recognize student teaching and related experiences as a joint responsibility of the teacher preparing institutions and the cooperating public schools through state provisions for:

a. minimum standards to guarantee adequacy of facilities and program of the public schools selected as laboratories for teacher-education activities;

b. minimum qualifications for public school teachers who direct the work of student teachers;

c. remuneration of public school districts serving as teacher-education laboratories;

d. remuneration of public school teachers, in addition to their contractual salaries, for their services in directing the activities of student teachers;

e. the development, coordination, and support of a cooperative program, involving many colleges and public schools, to provide special training for public school teachers and administrators who direct laboratory experiences for prospective teachers.

7. A cooperatively developed plan for establishing levels of preparation and experience for cooperating teachers. After an appropriate trial period, approved parts of such a program should be incorporated into

the official certification program of the state and used as a basis for remuneration of special teacher-education services.

8. Appropriate provision in the state school foundation program and
regular appropriation bills for special financial support for public schools
and teachers performing teacher-education services.

9. Legislation or official state regulations setting forth clearly the
legal status of student teachers and providing for agreements between
public school districts and colleges, together with proper controls for the
delegation of authority and liability.

The effectiveness of any major fraction of the above plan is
largely dependent upon defining some quality levels in teachers'
service for college students. A projection of a division of levels
designated as cooperating teacher, sponsor teacher, and teacher
education associate, is given in the 1959 Yearbook of the Association for Student Teaching.[3] Naturally this task is subject to much
the same obstacles as plans for merit pay for teachers, but the most
effective plans have used as their chief criteria special preparation
for this particular function, experience in giving the service, and
demonstrated competence as judged jointly by the college and the
public school authorities. Georgia's plan has no formal legal basis,
but is a cooperative undertaking of the State Department of Education, the public schools, and the collegiate institutions, and it includes three levels of preparation and three levels of payment by the
State Department. The supplementary payments are intended to
apply on travel and other expenses incurred by the cooperating
teacher in his work, or when qualifying for this responsibility.

A state plan for remuneration could consist of payments on only
one criteria or many; and when the schedule of payments is raised
to an appropriate level, it should take the place of monetary payments by colleges to public schools and teachers. A plan for support
for teacher-education laboratories might include payments of any
one or more of the following types:

1. To school districts based on the number of credit hours earned by
student teachers served in that district. (California pays $5 per semester
hour.)

2. To each teacher for each student teacher served, and based on the

---

[3] L. O. Andrews, "The Task Ahead," *The Supervising Teacher*, Thirty-Eighth
Yearbook (Cedar Falls, Iowa: The Association for Student Teaching, 1959) pp.
122–128.

teacher's status or certificate for this particular service. (Georgia pays $20 for the first level, $30 for the second level, and $50 for the third level. Other states have proposed a much higher scale.)

3. To each district to provide an extra increment regularly for each teacher who has reached the highest level, such as teacher education associate.

4. To each district for administrative and special services a percentage (perhaps 10 per cent) of the special payments to teachers of that district for teacher-education services.

5. To each district a specified amount (such as $1 for each student teacher) for school professional libraries for the use of cooperating teachers and student teachers.

6. To each district a number of additional teacher units (in proportion to the number of student teachers served) under a state foundation program to make possible a reduction of teacher loads giving time for conferences and supervisory service.

Descriptions and projections of quality programs are more common in the various states than any other features of this proposal; and some plan of standards for cooperating teachers exists in more than half of the states. Only a few of the latter, however, include formal certification requirements currently enforced. Comprehensive state plans, of either an official or unofficial type, have been developed recently in Minnesota, New Jersey, Ohio, Texas, Virginia, and Wisconsin; while Kentucky and North Carolina have very impressive publications incorporating the approved program approach to standards for teacher-education institutions. Most of these bulletins are the result of many months of cooperative study by representatives of the state department, colleges, and public schools. In several cases the state unit of the Association for Student Teaching played an active part in the work on these standards.

In 1963 the West Virginia legislature passed a bill revising a section of the school code including these provisions:

> The education of teachers . . . shall be under the general direction and control of the State Board of Education, which shall, through the State Superintendent of Schools, exercise supervisory control over teacher preparation programs in all institutions of higher education, including student teaching in the public schools, . . . the State Board of Education may enter into an agreement with county boards of education for the use of the public schools. Such agreement shall recognize student teaching as a joint responsibility of the teacher-preparation institution and the cooperating

public schools and shall include (1) the minimum qualifications for
the employment of public school teachers selected as supervising
teachers; (2) the remuneration to be paid public school teachers by
the State Board, in addition to their contractual salaries, for supervising student teachers; and (3) minimum standards to guarantee
adequacy of facilities and program of the public school selected for
student teaching.[4]

In his critical analysis of teacher education Conant devoted
much attention to student teaching, and his recommendations are
probably more penetrating and more comprehensive than those of
any other person not engaged in professional teacher education. In
addition to recommendations 4 and 18 quoted earlier, number 5
proposes that the state assume major responsibility for quality
programs:

> The state should approve programs of practice teaching. It
> should, working cooperatively with the college and public school
> authorities, regulate the conditions under which practice teaching
> is done and the nature of the methods instruction that accompanies
> it. The state should require that the colleges and public school sys-
> tems involved submit evidence concerning the competence of those
> appointed as cooperating teachers and clinical professors.[5]

Conant's third recommendation covers the schools' responsibility
for providing quality personnel for teacher-education activities:

> Public school systems that enter contracts with a college or uni-
> versity for practice teaching should designate, as classroom teach-
> ers working with practice teaching, only those persons in whose
> competence as teachers, leaders, and educators they have the high-
> est confidence, and should give such persons encouragement by re-
> ducing their work loads and raising their salaries.[6]

Following this recommendation Conant asserts:

> The acceptance of Recommendation 3 and its full implementa-
> tion would mean an increase in the budget. What I have in mind is
> a considerable raise in salary for the cooperating teacher.[7]

---

[4] Enrolled Committee Substitute for Senate Bill No. 37 (Passed March 7, 1963;
in effect ninety days from passage), West Virginia Legislature, Charleston, West
Virginia.

[5] James B. Conant, *The Education of American Teachers* (New York: McGraw-
Hill Book Company, 1963), pp. 64–65.

[6] *Ibid.*, p. 63.

[7] *Ibid.*, p. 63.

Immediately upon the release of the Conant book, New York's Commissioner of Education, James E. Allen, Jr., announced that he would request $500,000 in his next budget to be made available to school districts and colleges on a matching basis for improving student teaching.

These recent developments indicate that there is an increased understanding of the place and importance of student teaching. Perhaps many states will now consider proposals for action.

Possible Uses of the New Media

The educational possibilities of a library of teletape and sound film reproductions of real teaching situations was developed in Chapter II. Such a library could be a source of illustrative and study material for the widest variety of situations before, during, and after student teaching. An entirely new approach to the supervision of student teachers is being explored at Stanford University and Hunter College in the use of a newly perfected portable television tape recorder. It is still too early to predict the success of this approach, but the device does make it possible for a supervisor to sit with a student teacher and analyze an audio-visual recording of his performance, or to mail such a record back to his supervisor at a distant college.

Educators generally are agreed that the success of the teaching machine is dependent largely upon the quality of the programming. It is entirely conceivable that some of the most pertinent material on child growth and development, learning, and child and adolescent psychology could be put on programs for use with student teachers more or less on a remedial basis. Then when a cooperating teacher identified in his student teacher an area of inadequate understanding, the student could use the machine to review or add to his knowledge for immediate use back in the classroom.

Another issue in this area raises a very difficult question. Should a student teacher be assigned in a situation where a major part of his teaching experience would be in the use of the various new media, or should he have his experience in a less well-equipped situation closer to the type of school in which he will start teaching? With the normal life expectancy, many of the teachers graduated in the 1960's will be retiring around the year 2000. The changes they are likely to see during their careers stagger the imagination. It seems perfectly obvious that a major task of the teacher-education curriculum is to prepare beginning teachers to adjust to change. The student teacher needs to have had enough experience with the commonplace that he has acquired a readiness to use appropriate methods wisely and selectively with whatever materials are available, to experiment with the new, and to be able to discard the old when the new has proven superior. The rapid development of the new media makes this a good area in which to apply the above approach.

Future Prospects Through Research

At an informal meeting on February 26, 1950, at Atlantic City, over a score of persons heard reports of research studies that gave promise of a coming breakthrough in the long struggle to find a way to measure teacher effectiveness. As one result of that meeting, a succession of committees worked at the central problem, and, in 1963, the sponsoring organization, The American Educational Research Association, brought out its historic volume, edited by N. L. Gage, *Handbook on Research on Teaching*. While this massive volume, reporting on research in teaching from many different points of view, is not likely to have much immediate effect on practice in student teaching, its possible significance seems very great indeed for improvement in professional teacher education and, especially as a stimulant to improved research in all aspects of teacher education.

Although student teaching as such is not a separate category in the handbook, there are numerous studies reported of student teachers and student teaching. Some of the chapters of great interest and value for the worker in student teaching include: "6. Measuring classroom behavior by systematic observation; 7. Rating methods in research on teaching; 11. The teacher's personality and characteristics; 13. Social interaction in the classroom; and 14. The social background of teaching,"[8] plus nine chapters on research in separate subject areas or levels.

Findings from research on the nature of teaching appear in

[8] N. L. Gage, ed. *Handbook on Research in Teaching*, A Project of The American Educational Research Association (Chicago: Rand McNally and Company, 1963).

current studies, and four of the leaders are B. O. Smith, studying the nature of teaching; David G. Ryans, on teacher behavior; Marie Hughes, with her classification of teacher behavior; and Ned A. Flanders on the measurement of classroom climate. Evaluating the performance of student teachers through classroom observations has long been a controversial and difficult area of activity, but now, as demonstrated at the University of Minnesota,[9] research shows that it is possible to refine techniques to make even subjective judgments reliable enough to serve both operational and research purposes. Carefully trained observers with refined techniques have provided the data by which answers were obtained to very practical problems at Temple University and the University of Miami.

Speaking to the Fort Collins Workshop of the Association for Student Teaching in 1962, Ianni drew this pertinent distinction:

> Behavioral science, and consequently research in the behavioral sciences, has always been framed within a very strict concept of objectivity. Thus, the behavioral scientist tends to describe what *is,* rather than what *ought* to be. Education, on the other hand, is an active process, and, consequently, the educational researcher and the educator are constantly faced with the task of describing *what* ought to be as well as what is.[10]

This quotation neatly sums up the dilemma of the worker in student teaching—he must be able to make use of the results of a wide range of theoretical research, while at the same time developing sufficient skill to carry on extensive research in the whole range of the laboratory aspects of teacher education; and then he must be able to devise action research that will help practitioners to put both types to the test of use. Finally, to make the circle complete, the result of the last two steps should be some refined hypotheses that can be used as the basis for more theoretical as well as applied research.

Lindsey and her colleagues working with teachers at three dif-

---

[9] Roger E. Wilk and William H. Edson, with Don Davies and Naomi C. Chase, *A Study of the Relationship between Observed Classroom Behavior of Elementary Student Teachers.* Predictors of those Behaviors, and Ratings by Supervisors (College of Education, University of Minnesota, 1962).

[10] Francis A. J. Ianni, "The Contribution of Behavioral Science to Research in Teacher Education," *Research and Professional Experiences in Teacher Education,* Bulletin Number 20 (Cedar Falls, Iowa: The Association for Student Teaching, 1963), p. 9.

ferent institutions carried out a cooperative action research, which indicates the way to procedures and instrumentation that will make it possible for teachers and student teachers to benefit from new research findings.[11]

Some of the current research, which may prove to be the most important for student teaching, is concerned with the self-concept of the student teacher, role definitions, interpersonal relations, the lessening of anxieties, and mental health. In the latter field, two major projects in relation to student teaching and mental health have been carried on at the University of Texas and at San Francisco State College. Near the conclusion of the latter project, sponsored by the National Institute of Mental Health, Fred T. Wilhelms and Alice E. Siemons reported as follows to a section of the Columbus TEPS Conference in June of 1963:

> More important than quantity are the quality of the experience, appropriateness to the individual needs of the student, range and variety in grade levels and schools, and identification of varying purposes for experience depending on the student's previous background.
> . . . two general observations: First, spreading a variety of experiences with children and youth in school and community over the whole period of professional preparation is superior to concentrating nearly all of it toward the end as student teaching.
> Second, experience must be conceived as far more than practice . . . The development of a true experience program is exceedingly intricate. Not all students need the same elements or proportions of elements. Timing is important to get theory and experience into two-way reinforcement.
> . . . the possible patterns of experience are virtually infinite . . . the changeover from college student into professional teacher is deeply personal . . . [a] great period of personal growth and self-forming.

Thus these recent studies are beginning to present research evidence in support of dimensions and qualities of student teaching that have been advocated for many years. At last it appears that a breakthrough is in progress which will affect student teaching. But in summarizing this whole field of research Lynch sounds a note of

---

11 Margaret Lindsey, Leslie Mauth, and Edith Groteberg, *Improving Laboratory Experiences in Teacher Education* (New York: Bureau of Publications, Teachers College, Columbia University, 1959).

caution while at the same time pointing out some desirable guides for further effort:

> Let us not be deluded into thinking that more and better verbalized knowledge about psychology on the one hand, or extensive field experience on the other, will, *per se,* result in more insightful perception and greater effectiveness in interpersonal relations. The learnings involved are too intricate to permit us to trust simply to more knowledge or to sheer, raw experience in the real situation. Rather, what seems to be needed is carefully guided experience, starting with simple situations, with ample opportunities for trial and correction in practice. The fact that values so permeate perception further suggests that more attention to the learning of values is needed in teacher education.[12]

In reviewing the whole range of recent developments, including the small sampling reported here, several observations seem pertinent. Davies points up the need for a team approach in this way:

> Few individuals in education combine in one person all the understanding and skill needed to conduct research today. A team approach is obviously needed. We need classroom teachers in schools and colleges who are skillful in identifying the problems that need study; we need philosophers and theoreticians who can set problems in proper context and provide value yardsticks against which the results of research can be measured; we need experts in research design; we need statisticians; we need technicians who will be able to utilize the mechanical and electronic aids to analysis; and we need skillful administrators who can facilitate the work of all of these others. If this notion of a team approach is accepted, then those of us who lack certain skills need no longer shrink from research endeavors.[13]

Doctoral dissertations in teacher education, produced by teams of two or more graduate students at Teachers College, Columbia University, represent an interesting application of this approach.

Individual research effort carried on with personal funds is just not adequate to attempt the kind of projects that so need attention.

---

[12] William W. Lynch, Jr., "Interpersonal Perception: A Neglected Aspect of Teaching," *Theory Into Practice,* Vol. II, No. 2 (Columbus, Ohio: Bureau of Educational Research and Service, College of Education, The Ohio State University), p. 94.

[13] Don Davies, "Research in Teacher Education: Nature, Classification, and Evaluation," *Leadership Through Research,* Research Bulletin, Number 4 (Cedar Falls, Iowa: The Association for Student Teaching, 1961), p. 10.

Thus, it is fortunate that foundations and the federal government under the Cooperative Research Program of the Office of Education as well as other agencies are providing increasingly substantial sums for research in teacher education. Under these conditions it may now be possible to make longitudinal case studies of many aspects of the growth of a prospective teacher from high school days through the first few years of professional service. This approach seems well adapted to learning much from study of the professional and personal problems of those who prove not well adapted to teaching. Many supervisors have discovered subjectively that their experiences in working with very pathological student-teacher cases have given them clues and hypotheses to apply and test with students in the more normal ranges of ability and success.

Challenge to the Profession

As research findings begin to accumulate, the next logical step will be to set up well-supported demonstration centers for the application and testing of these concepts and hypotheses in regular program situations. This will place a new burden upon the schools serving as teacher-education laboratories, but one which can be managed if reasonable support is forthcoming. But this additional demand to be placed on the public schools highlights very sharply the importance of solving at an early date the operational problems, which have been presented in detail in this book. The operational problems can be solved, but it will take vigorous effort on the part of the profession as a whole plus adequate financial support to get the job done.

The news media continually bombard the public with the facts of the expansion of knowledge and the accelerating pace of change. In the past, student teaching and the whole area of professional experiences for the prospective teacher have shown a stubborn resistance to rapid change, and, indeed, often, resistance to much discernible improvement for considerable periods of time. The ingredients for producing significant change loom on the horizon, but unfortunately they may not actually come along in just the right sequence.

The task of the profession for the immediate future, then, is to take the best thinking of the experienced leaders in the field, to develop a set of goals and guiding principles, to rally the influential elements of the profession, to work for the needed legislation and support, to raise the quality to the highest levels possible with the means at hand—all the time utilizing the best of the research information as it becomes available.

As a concurrent operation, support must be found for the development of an extensive theoretical background for the many facets of this field and all of teacher education. The results of basic research in education and the related disciplines can then be used as a means of developing hypotheses for testing the theoretical projections. From this point the applied research and action research can take over to feed the results back into the ongoing process.

Perhaps the most important lesson to be learned from these recent developments is that the profession doesn't have to wait for new legislation, new certification patterns, new standards, new tried and proven methods. Using the best that is known goals can be set now. As various aspects of these goals prove useful in practice, they can be written into laws, developed into standards, and shared as sound procedures. In this way the professional aspects of teacher education can be made a much more effective pathway into the profession, and one which will be broad, challenging, effective, and satisfying for those who choose to prepare for their life work in teaching.

Bibliography

Since 1937 The Association for Student Teaching has included in its yearbooks an annual bibliography of publications on student teaching and related laboratory experiences. Prepared by advanced doctoral students at Teachers College, Columbia University, under the direction of Dr. Florence Stratemeyer, these classified and annotated lists provide the best single source of information on writings in this field. The bibliography given below includes some of the most significant references and the primary continuing sources of current publications on student teaching. Omitted from the listing are the many textbooks for student teachers and the great number and variety of local, institutional, and state manuals, handbooks, bulletins, workbooks, and guides.

HISTORICAL

Armentrout, Winfield D., *The Conduct of Student Teaching in State Teachers Colleges*. Greeley, Colorado: Colorado State Teachers College, 1927.

Learned, William S. and William C. Bagley, *The Professional Preparation of Teachers for American Schools*. New York: The Carnegie Foundation for the Advancement of Teaching, 1920.

Mead, Arthur R., *Supervised Student-Teaching*. Richmond: Johnson Publishing Company, 1930.

The Education of Teachers, Yearbook XXIII of the National Society of College Teachers of Education. Chicago: The University of Chicago Press, 1935.

The Sub-Committee of the Standards and Surveys Committee, *School and Community Laboratory Experiences in Teacher Education*. Oneonta, New York: The American Association of Teachers Colleges, 1948.

Williams, E. I. F., *The Actual and Potential Use of Laboratory Schools in State Normal Schools and Teachers Colleges*. New York: Bureau of Publications, Teachers College, Columbia University, 1942.

RECENT GENERAL WORKS

Conant, James B., *The Education of American Teachers*. New York: McGraw Hill Book Company, 1963.

Cottrell, Donald P., ed., *Teacher Education for a Free People*. Oneonta, New York: The American Association of Colleges for Teacher Education, 1956.

Gage, N. L., *Handbook of Research on Teaching,* A Project of the American Educational Research Association. Chicago: Rand McNally & Co. 1963.

Lindsey, Margaret, ed., *New Horizons for the Teaching Profession.* Washington, D.C.: The National Commission on Teacher Education and Professional Standards, 1961.

Lindsey, Margaret, Leslie Mauth, and Edith Groteberg, *Improving Laboratory Experiences in Teacher Education.* New York: Bureau of Publications, Teachers College, Columbia University, 1959.

McGeoch, Dorothy M., *Direct Experiences in Teacher Education: A Story of Three Programs.* New York: Bureau of Publications, Teachers College, Columbia University, 1953.

Steeves, Frank D., *Issues in Student Teaching.* New York: The Odyssey Press, Inc., 1963.

Wiggins, Samuel P., *The Student Teacher in Action.* Boston: Allyn and Bacon, Inc., 1957.

Woodruff, Asahel D., *Student Teaching Today.* Washington, D.C.: The American Association of Colleges for Teacher Education, 1960.

YEARBOOKS

Selected yearbooks of The Association for Student Teaching, Cedar Falls, Iowa:

The Evaluation of Student Teaching, 1949
Off-Campus Student Teaching, 1951
Facilities for Professional Laboratory Experiences in Teacher Education, 1954
Functions of Laboratory Schools in Teacher Education, 1955
Four Went to Teach, 1956
Guidance in Teacher Education, 1957
The Supervising Teacher, 1959
Evaluating Student Teaching, 1960
Teacher Education and the Public Schools, 1961
Outlook in Student Teaching, 1962
Concern for the Individual in Student Teaching, 1963

FOR COOPERATING TEACHERS

Curtis, Dwight K. and L. O. Andrews, *Guiding Your Student Teacher.* Englewood Cliffs, New Jersey: Prentice-Hall, Inc., 1954.

Haines, Aleyne C., *Guiding the Student Teaching Process in Elementary Education.* Chicago: Rand McNally & Company, 1960.

Milner, Ernest J., *You and Your Student Teacher.* New York: Bureau of Publications, Teachers College, Columbia University, 1954.

Stratemeyer, Florence V. and Margaret Lindsey, *Working With Student Teachers.* New York: Bureau of Publications, Teachers College, Columbia University, 1958.

OTHER CONTINUING SOURCES

Bulletin Series, The Association for Student Teaching, Cedar Falls, Iowa.
Reasearch Bulletin Series, The Association for Student Teaching, Cedar
    Falls, Iowa.
Journal of Teacher Education
Educational Administration and Supervision

Index

Index

DATE DUE

MAR 1 8 '65			
APR 1 '65			
DEC 0 '65			
MAR 1 1 1970			
SEP 2 3 1975			
DEC 0 8 1989			
FEB 2 8 1991			
GAYLORD			PRINTED IN U.S.A.